BEYOND THE
COBBLESTONES

BEYOND THE COBBLESTONES

BY LUISA LIVORNO
RAMONDO

NEW DEGREE PRESS

COPYRIGHT © 2021 LUISA LIVORNO RAMONDO

BEYOND THE COBBLESTONES

ISBN   978-1-63730-619-2   *Hardcover*

978-1-63676-880-9   *Paperback*

978-1-63676-881-6   *Kindle Ebook*

978-1-63676-882-3   *Ebook*

DEDICATION

———

To my husband, Damien, for always making life so colorful,
and loving me through thick and thin.

To Luke for your sweet soul, to Damien for your immense strength,
and to Giordan for your irresistible personality.
You are all the true loves of my life!

To my parents, Antonietta & Leonardo, whose lives inspired this
book and continue to inspire me every day.

To all my friends and family for helping me get this far, especially the
strong, smart women that I am blessed to have in my life.

AND

To all the young girls out there with big dreams...
never let anything get in your way!

CONTENTS

———

AUTHOR'S NOTE

When I started this book many years ago, I hadn't had any earth-shattering experiences or life changing events that led me to write this story.

No "ah-ha" moments.

No revelations.

No lightbulbs coming on over my head.

Instead, it was steady little bits of information that started as far back as my memory goes. Little details, stories told over the years, traditions I didn't understand but followed, time spent with relatives in two different countries; all sparked the writing of this story.

It was like a small child, clawing at me, needing my attention.

As a family, we started off in a row home in East Falls. It is an unassuming little town in Philadelphia, Pennsylvania, close to the Schuylkill River where I went for picnics with my mother. My parents owned a small supermarket in our town that primarily serviced the low-income housing community nearby. It was a tough neighborhood, and I was different from everyone around me, and that wasn't a good combination.

I learned very quickly that being accepted as an American in America wasn't a given, and I wanted to be more American. I wanted to have an American-sounding name, like Jennifer or Michelle. I wanted to have American parents who knew how to speak English properly and how to make a peanut butter and jelly sandwich with white bread. These may seem like insignificant struggles to you, but growing up different is what kids often dread.

All we want to do is be like everybody else when we're young, and we never realize at the time that it's a good thing that we're not.

My brother, sister, and I were taught from a very young age that you work for everything you want, and you certainly don't let what other people think get in the way of your dreams. We grew up surrounded by love, laughs, and lots of hard work, and we knew deep in our core that hard work would pay off.

Of course, we struggled.

My parents didn't speak English very well, so we were considered weird in our very American neighborhood.

I was bullied at a very young age because my family was different.

I was embarrassed by the food I brought to school, so I would throw it in the trash and pretend I forgot my lunch.

These struggles at times made me regret my heritage, and I often wished I had a different life.

However, as I matured, I began to understand how fortunate we were to be here. To have the opportunity to work and buy a home, to build something of value for our family. I grew up most of my life well aware of the struggles that my parents went through to get to this country. Then, I was constantly reminded of the struggles my parents went through to keep what we earned in this country. Even though we didn't have much, I spent a lot of time around people who had less. That, coupled with the many stories I heard of their childhoods, finally led me down a road of gratitude and appreciation.

My parents' history was what led me to the understanding that we were lucky to be in America. They shared stories about a country that everyone romanticizes and admires for its beauty. And beautiful it is! Even though my parents shared many stories of arduous lives growing up, they both admit to being content in what they knew at the time, surrounded by a loving family and a loving country.

However, no matter how beautiful and romantic Italy was, my mother knew they would never get anywhere there.

Through much planning, saving, and waiting years through the immigration process, they moved away from everything they knew for what was sure to be a better life in the unknown. They had no money, didn't speak the language, and had limited family to rely on in their new country.

But America was the place to be.

And they were determined to get there. This was ingrained in my head from birth. No matter how bad it ever gets here, it's always better than anywhere else in the world. At some point, I started to think that people who were born and raised here, and had many generations of family who were born and raised here, didn't feel this same appreciation. I learned to see this country through the eyes of my parents, and it is a view that I have never lost.

My parents' stories of hard times, poverty, and lack of opportunity are what drove my mother to move her family to this country. My father followed, reluctantly, but a day doesn't go by when he isn't grateful for her determination. He is of the opinion that life in this country has turned out, by far, to be better than any life they would've had in Italy. They are proud of what they have achieved here, and I'm incredibly proud of them for taking such considerable chances.

I often try to imagine what my life would have been like if my parents had never come here, or worse, if they had come here and decided to go back because things were too difficult. Some of their friends did that back then. Sometimes it was easier to go back to what you knew, but my parents did not.

They stayed on a very difficult path in order to give our family the opportunities they didn't have when they were growing up.

This is a story about a girl in a small Italian town who has the spark from a very young age to be more than that small town would've allowed.

It is a depiction of the dream my mother had for a better life and all the years I lived growing up in that dream.

It is my belief you will see that no matter how difficult things may seem, or how many obstacles stand in your way, that if you persevere, you can make your dreams come true.

PROLOGUE

I'm an old woman now, but I was once young like you.

I was born in Orsara di Puglia, a small town in the South of Italy, about eighty-three square kilometers in size, population 3,200. The streets were small and made of stone. The hills were brutal, but the weather was kind to us. Except the north wind. That was a mean wind, and when she blew, it felt like little knives piercing your skin. As luck would have it, we were blessed with the warmth of the sun and very mild days for most of the year.

We spent a lot of time outside, on the cobblestone streets. We talked to our neighbors, about things like war, religion, and food; and of course there was always town gossip. I remember having lots of friends around all the time. We lived poorly, and in tight quarters, so people were always close. Nothing was private. Everyone knew your business, but I didn't mind that too much.

The real beauty was that a lot of people in our town were in the same situation as we were, so everything seemed normal. We walked everywhere, including the places we could fill our water buckets and get wood for the fire; we also had to do our laundry outside. We did this with our friends, since they had to do the same chores, anyway, and we had fun doing it. It may seem strange to you that laundry would be fun, but it was. Playing at the fountain, splashing each other, and laughing over who lost the battle and had to wash their clothes downstream made a boring, everyday chore seem like a game to us.

It was a good life, or so we thought.

Life was simple then, and even when I go back, it's still the same in a lot of ways.

Of course, people have modern conveniences now like machines to wash their clothes, but dryers are not common. Walk through town, and you'll see sheets hanging out to dry from every balcony, swaying in the breeze, warm from the sun. The people who live on the main roads are lucky, since the streets are wider and the sun is able to shine through. My house was on a street where the sun didn't make it through quite as easily.

The sounds of the streets made my heart sing with happiness.

The church bells of San Nicola di Bari would ring every day, and it was a welcomed expression of our obligations to *Chiesa Madre*. The Mother Church reminded us that we were a family, and we had to take care of each other.
And we did.

Everyone in town helped each other out if they could.

Children would run through the streets, sometimes barefoot, feet hitting against the cobblestones and echoing between the buildings. Voices carrying through the little alleyways. Whistles and singing, laughing and mothers screaming, these are all the sounds I remember growing up.

Sounds of joy, sounds of despair, sounds of responsibility; all of it stirs up memories for me.

We had no money, very little food, and nowhere to go.

But one thing was true: even though we didn't have much, we had our community, and we had our country.

Our traditions were rich and strong. We followed them like a map through our lives, always guiding us through the years, teaching us about who we are. And one thing I can say for sure is that Italians know themselves. They don't always share what they feel, but they always know who they are inside at their core. And for me that began in that little town. This is how I was raised.

So, when you read my story, I hope you realize that it was hard, but it was good. Good in that we were loved, we were challenged, we knew who we were, and we knew that with hard work we could have a better life than those who came before us.

It's the early years of my life that shaped me into the person I am today, and no matter how grim it may sound on these pages, I am forever grateful.

CHAPTER 1

───

I need to get away from everyone.

I like to daydream about what exists outside of this town. I have to believe it's a big world out there. I see movies on the television down at the neighborhood bar. I see what's in the newspapers.

I know there's more out there.

A whole big world, away from here.

My street, Via Silvio Pellico, isn't actually a street, but an alley about five feet wide that you can only go through on foot or bike. The sun is blocked by the cold stone houses and doesn't make it through very much. The temperature is cool most of the time since everything is made of stone. It's nice in the summer, but not so much in the winter. Most of the surrounding streets are like that, which makes having a car useless since you would have to park somewhere else in town and walk all the way to your house, anyway.

Not that having a car is an option.

We have no money and there are no cars in Orsara.

On Via Silvio Pellico, we live on the ground level at number thirty-one, which has a blue door. The lower levels host doors to enter the houses, and long flights of steps lead to houses on the second levels. Eleven of us live in this small, two-room house with no windows other than the one on the door. I can't say that it's very comfortable, but it's a place to live, and it's ours.

When you walk into my house, there's a long, narrow hallway with a water barrel on the right.

It is my job to keep this barrel full.

On the left is a pen for our pig. This time his name is Pepe.

We will keep him here for a few months and then kill him so we have food for the winter.

"Claudia," Mama says, quietly annoyed, "go and fetch the water now! We need to make the pasta early today. I have a lot to do, and your father will be home tonight." She says it urgently, trying not to wake the whole house.

It's Spring, and my father is coming home from one of his work rotations out of town. My mother always wants to be ready for when he comes home. It's usually a happy night since he comes with money, but not always.

My older sister Paola already went out to get firewood, so I was definitely lagging behind schedule.

"Okay, Mama," I say as I hurry out to get water, one of my many duties.

Walking down the alley, I see some neighbors congregating outside to gossip. This is their typical morning routine. Signora Russo is in the middle of them, as usual, in command of the day's stories.

"Claudia, where are you going?" asks Signora Russo.

"I have to get the water." I keep walking as I say it, hoping she won't ask me any more questions. She always wants to know everything.

I hate getting the water. Day in and day out I have to get water. I always dream about what it would be like to live in a house where you have water running into a sink.

It's impossible to even imagine.

As I return with the water, I call to my mother. "Mama, I'm back!"

While dumping the water into the large barrel, it splashes with a refreshing sound that I love, knowing I am now done fetching water for today.

"Good. Now let's start making the pasta."

I walk one step down to the kitchen table and sit back in a chair as I spy the embers in the *fornacella*, creating just enough light for us to work. This little oven is the heart of our home. Not just for cooking, but for heat, too.

Near the oven is a *fazzatora* to make the dough in. It's made of wood and shaped like a small boat. I get the grain out of the contraption built into the middle of the wall and start to crush it into a powdery mess. I form the powder into the shape of a volcano and then I add water to the center. I begin by methodically forming the powder into a dough, always working toward the middle. The sides of the fazzatora are slanted away from the center, so I play with the mixture by moving it up and down on each side, rhythmically, to the music in my head.

"Claudia, come on!" My mother's patience is wearing thin. I understand it's time to stop playing with the mixture, so I mix and mix and knead and knead, all the while listening to the music in my head and daydreaming about anything and nothing. The dough is forming quickly into a nice round ball and is springy to the touch. It is ready for Mama.

This is the way it's always been; I can't remember anything different. We make dough for pasta and bread. Tradition runs deep here, and everyone does it. I don't understand why it's so important, but I think it may be because most of us are poor and it's too expensive to buy pasta already made. Mama says that pasta making is an art. Well, certain pastas, anyway.

When we make orecchiette or cicatelli, then it's definitely an art. Fettuccini is easy—anyone can do that.

I walk away from the fazzatora so my mother can take over. She cuts the dough into smaller pieces, rolls out each piece in long, pencil-like strings, and begins to make cicatelli, my favorite pasta.

"Mama, what are you making the pasta with tonight?" I ask.

"I picked some greens from the town field that I can use. Go wash them and cut them up," Mama says as she hands me the bucket of greens.

"Okay," I say, a little disappointed that we weren't having cicatelli with tomatoes. I'm so sick of greens from the field. But we don't have any tomatoes, and it's not worth fighting with Mama, so I keep my mouth shut.

No one has anything to call their own in our house, so we learn to share from an early age. We sleep on large sacks filled with corn husks, all the kids together on a wooden platform built above my parents' bed. We have one dresser to keep our family clothes in and one lightbulb hanging by a wire in the center of the room.

I go outside with the bucket of greens and sit on a neighbor's step since my house doesn't have one. I carefully pick the little bugs out of the greens and clip the ends off with my fingers. The day is just beginning, and the smell coming from the neighbor's house is delicious.

One of my neighbors has some figs and nuts on their little roof out to dry. I take a couple and put them in my pocket for later. We do this sometimes, my sister Paola and I. They never yell at us. Maybe they don't notice or maybe they don't mind since they know we're so poor.

"Claudia, let's go!" My mother bellows out our front door for help with dinner and the children, but I ignore her for now. In addition to my older sister, I have six younger brothers and sisters. My mother is pregnant every year and I hate it. Every time she's going to have another baby, I see it as more work for me. It's embarrassing, too; we're so poor we can hardly feed ourselves, and yet she keeps having babies. I wish she would stop.

My mother is a mystery. Her name is Josefina Curcio, and she was born poor like me. I guess poverty is one of those things that gets handed down from generation to generation. She's rough, not pretty by any stretch of the imagination, with dark brown hair. Her face is hard looking, eyes dark and lips always pursed in disgust. She's a big-boned woman, her shape that of a pear but hard as a rock. She has given birth ten times already, which I guess explains the constant scowl on her face.

I don't know what her dreams are. She never speaks about anything other than chores.

Make the pasta, get the water, watch the children, sweep the floor.

One after another she barks them out.

She is never at a loss for speaking, but I feel like I really don't know anything about her.

Nevertheless, she has the babies, that is her life.

I think she's very smart, and I see a glimmer of ambition in her, yet somehow, she fell in love with a man who doesn't have the same aspirations in life that she does. My father's name is Angelo Valentino, and he isn't around much. He has a hard time finding work, but he says it's a difficult time out there. So he does odd jobs in town for extra food or money—that is, when he's not on a rotation.

Like if the handle falls off your ladle, he can fix that. I love my father; he's a simple man, kind, and I have to believe he's doing his best.

"Claudia!" I hear my mother calling me with more urgency.

"Coming, Mama!" I keep my eyes to the ground as I carry the bucket back to the house, being careful not to step on the lines between the cobblestones. I'm walking on my toes, tapping each stone lightly as I go.

I know I will get out of this town, but how? Life is so complicated here. We have so many kids in our house, and all I am is another helping hand. Days are always the same: get up, do chores, help the younger kids get dressed, make breakfast, and go to school. It isn't the life I want. Except the school part.

Suddenly, I'm ripped from my thoughts by blood-curdling screams.

"Oh Dio, oh Dio, no, no, no…" Crying uncontrollably, my mother speaks these words that I know I will never forget. A haunting, scary sound that you never want to hear coming out of your mother's mouth.

"Mama, what, what's going on?" But I already know. I know what the sound of her cries are saying even before the words come out. It's a sound you recognize even the first time you hear it. The sound of complete desperation and tragedy.

My mother drops to her knees in a pain that I can't even imagine.

"Oh Dio, e morto!" My mother is clutching a little baby all wrapped up in a blanket frayed from years of use. I couldn't see which one it was.

The twins were the most recent babies born to my mother. Two boys named Giuseppe and Franco. They were born in the winter, just a few months ago. It was colder than cold and late at night when the midwife came to help my mother.

Franco was the first to be born and a sad-looking creature he was. He came out very small, and very weak. Being born at home didn't help his situation much, and we were sure he wouldn't make it through the night. But he did, and, still not convinced he was going to survive, we had both babies baptized immediately. My mother was so afraid he would die that there was no time to spare.

Giuseppe, on the other hand, was born healthy, big and solid; he looked like an ox. He had a smile that could open up your heart, and we could tell he was going to be strong.

"Oh Dio, Giuseppe, NO!" All of sudden, a couple of neighbors come in and I stand in awe of this dreadful scene unfolding before my eyes. Giuseppe? How could he die? He's so healthy and strong, it just doesn't make any sense.

"Mama, let me see, Mama!" I need to see his face. She could be confused.

His face is so pale it's almost light blue. His lips are dark, and he has no expression. I start crying. It's never a good thing to see a dead baby. My brothers and sisters are all waking up and starting to realize what is going on. I can see fear in their little faces.

"Claudia what's..." My sister Lidia wants to know. She is sitting on the bed with my sister Elena and the boys. I look at her sharply, and she knows to close her mouth. We can't answer questions right now.

"Oh, Mama, it is Giuseppe!" Just like that I hear the cries of the other twin, screaming for attention. I rush over to pick up Franco, and he's okay. He calms down and stops crying, and I grab one of the bottles my mother had prepared to feed the babies. He latches on to it immediately, and all was right with him. Even though he looks sickly and weak, he is thriving.

Signora Russo and a couple of other women come in. "What's going on? What's wrong?" they ask, but the minute they see my mother crying on the floor with a baby in her arms, they know. Dead babies are not uncommon in a poor little town like ours.

The women pick my mother up off the floor and help her tend to the body. I take Franco and the other kids outside as Paola finally comes back from fetching wood and gets wind of the news.

"What's going on, what's happening?" She sounds a little frantic but unsure.

"Giuseppe died." I whisper so not to further upset the little ones, standing quietly, listening to the drama unfold among the adults in the house.

"Oh my God! Why? How did he die?" Paola is hysterical.

"I don't know, Paola. You know how sometimes babies die. It just happens, I guess." I find a seat on a neighbor's step to feed Franco while the other little ones sit around me. They don't know what to do, so they're clinging to me. Quietly, their little minds are trying to understand. Paola goes inside to help the ladies with my mother.

Giuseppe wasn't the first of my mother's babies to die at night. She lost two others that way, before I was born. I never heard anyone scream such pain before, and I hope I never have to hear that sound again.

That night, as my father returns, he hears the news on his way through town. As soon as he enters the room, he goes to my mother and holds her for longer than I've ever seen before. There's an understanding that families have with one another, and all of us in the room behave for the night

Everything is eerily quiet. Different from other nights.

There's no chatter, coughing, crying, snoring, kids running in circles, grunts of Pepe in the corner.

Even he knows to be quiet.

It's cold in the house, and I'm lucky to have a few minutes of peace by the fire. I watch the blue and orange flame, so vibrant and hopeful like a fire wants to be. It pops and crackles so loudly that it sounds like a firecracker in our small space. I want to touch the flames, see what they feel like. Can I grab it and hold it?

Everyone else is sleeping, so they don't notice the noise of the fire. I can't sleep, and the sound of it relaxes me, makes me happy, makes me forget that I am hungry.

Makes me forget that my little brother died today.

The peace I feel from the fire is starting to vanish, and my thoughts make me feel restless. I wonder how Giuseppe's twin brother will survive without him? I imagine it's true what they say about twins, and I worry Franco will forever have a void where Giuseppe should have been.

I don't think I'll ever be the same after that, either.

This day makes me realize I have to get away from this pitiful life.

As soon as possible.

CHAPTER 2

———

As I sit on the earth in the grotto, I find myself wishing I was anywhere but here. I would rather be in the stinky bathroom in school. It always has such an awful smell, but right now that would be better.

And I can't stop picturing Giuseppe's blue little face in my mind. It's been a few months since he died, but I can't stop thinking about him.

It's summertime, and I thank God for that!

Summer is my favorite time of year. Gardens are blooming all around, so food is less scarce, and the warmth of the sun is a gift after spending months being cold.

But the cool, wet grotto is where I am stuck today. The small cave has stone walls and a dirt floor and is just at the bottom of town, at the base of San Michele Arcangelo Church. Other families come, too. But not all. Some go to underground caves below the town churches. And some stay home because they say they're not hiding from anyone, especially not the Germans.

We walk down early in the morning and sit in the cave all day, and then we walk back to our house at night. This is how it's been for a while because of the war. Not all the time, just when we know there's a real threat coming.

Days in the grotto are depressing ones.

But sometimes, days we go to the grotto lead to visits at my grandmother's farm. Nonna's house isn't too far from there, maybe a fifteen-minute walk. It's welcoming and warm and we love to spend time there. The trees are beautiful, swaying gently in the cool breeze. The smell is pleasant, too, basil and tomatoes, garlic and onion; all these beautiful smells excite my nose and my stomach.

Nonna has a stone farmhouse that she got when she married her second husband, Martino. He has two older sons, but they don't live with him anymore. He's a wonderful man, very calm and nice. He is tall with long, dark hair. A little lanky, but there's something about him that I like. He always treats me nicely. He knows we have little food and always offers me something to eat.

"Claudia, are you hungry?" he asks me one day while at the farm.

This question makes me laugh inside because I'm always hungry.

And I don't dare laugh out loud; I certainly don't want to offend him.

"No, not really," I answer, embarrassed about being hungry, so I lie.

"Well, take some of these blackberries, anyway. I picked too many this morning, and they'll just go to waste. Maybe you can give them to your little brothers and sisters," he says.

"Sure, I guess, if you want me to." I act indifferent, but really I can't wait to get my hands on them. As soon as I'm alone, I swallow them up so quickly and savor every last bite of the sweet berries. I dream about them, which is what you do when you're hungry and poor and embarrassed.

You dream about food.

You obsess about food.

Nonna and Papa Martino have lots of animals, and they have one particular animal I love, their horse. Her name is Stella, and she has a white patch on her head that is shaped like a star. She's the most beautiful thing I have ever seen. Her body is golden, and she looks for me when I come to see her. Sometimes I sit in her stall at the end of the day, just studying her body and trying to connect with her. She's a beautiful mountain of strength.

Their house is big with plenty of room for all of us, which is different from what I'm accustomed to. Nonna's kitchen is warm, and her cooking thrills my senses. She never lacks for food as far as I can tell, which is probably why I like going there so much, even if she didn't have anything good to say about my mother and father.

But today we don't have enough time to even think about a visit to Nonna's. It's a bad day, so we rush into the grotto.

My mother hurries us in, me and Paola, and my brothers and sisters. The cave is dark and musty, and some of the other people from town are already there. It's roomy enough for all of us to hang out in for the day. I run my fingers along the wall with my eyes closed, feeling the bumpy coldness of the rocks. I can't see very clearly, but the walls seem like a light gray color, almost like something white leaked down over the dark rocks and stuck there. I sit on the earth, and quickly the world around me begins to fade away.

I get lost inside that cave. Not really lost, of course, since the cave is not that big. I mean, in my mind I get lost. That day, I sit on the ground and feel the damp earth below me, wetting my dress. I lean back against the rocks and close my eyes, and there it is, the sea! I find myself looking at this beautiful, blue body of water in my mind, and it is so calming. I have a red bathing suit on, and I am running toward the water. I feel the gritty sand under my feet, and soon the water is running through my toes.

What a beautiful day it is on the beach!

I imagine lots of people around, the sun is strong, and all the bodies are brown. As soon as I get to the water, I dive in headfirst and swim right down toward the bottom. There I see rocks and shells, and even some small fish swimming around frantically. The sun is glistening through the water, and shiny rays of light reflect off their little bodies.

It is a beautiful sight!

As I reach out to grab a fish, I hear my mother calling my name. "Claudia!" she exclaims. "Help me with him, please." As quickly as I went into my dream world, I am ripped out of it by the rough sound of my mother's voice. Franco was restless, and I could always calm him down.

We sit there for hours and hours, and the younger kids hate it. Mama brings some fruit and water, but it's still miserable. The Germans are a huge threat to us, and I don't understand why they bomb us in small towns. What have we done to make them so angry? No one seems to know, so we just try to stay out of sight.

This time we spend all day crouched down in the grotto. Once the bombing stops, we wait a little longer just to be sure it doesn't start up again, and then we run out into the field. Freedom.

"Claudia, look at this! I can't believe it!" says Paola.

"What now?" I ask with little interest. My sister always exaggerates. She makes a big deal out of everything, and most of the time it isn't anything great. So, I walk over to where she is, and there it lies, shiny, mangled, streaked with red paint and black smoke.

"Paola, do you know what that is?" I ask my sister, wondering if she can figure it out.

She ignores me, mesmerized by what she sees.

As she reaches for it, I grab her wrist, "No! It's too hot, don't touch it." The piece of metal lies there out of place in the field. We've found pieces of planes before, but none so new to the field as this.

"Well, what should we do with it?" she asks.

"Nothing, just leave it here. We can tell Papa Martino, in case he wants it. It's his land, anyway. Come on, let's go. I'm tired of being here, and we need to make dinner," I say to Paola to get her to move quickly.

My sister and I are friends, but we are very different. She loves me a lot and tries to take care of me, since she's older. We're the closest of the siblings since we're the two oldest and the most responsible. But sometimes I feel like I'm the older one.

We walk home in the dim evening light. School is about to begin, and I find myself excited about that, despite having spent the day in the grotto. I love going to school.

We get home in time to whip up a quick meal of stale bread, potatoes and some greens cooked in a broth. Sometimes we add white beans to this, but not tonight. We don't have any beans left.

I go to bed unsatisfied but happy with the anticipation of what tomorrow will bring.

———

The time has finally come!

I wake up feeling excited and scared all at once. It's the first day of school, and I can't wait to go. Mama doesn't make us do our morning chores on the first day of school, so I get up and quickly start getting ready. I have a pink and white checkered uniform apron with buttons on the back. It is my favorite piece of clothing, and the only pink I own. My white shirt that I wear underneath the apron is clean and fresh. I have lamb's wool tights that I knitted myself with an opening in the middle, so I don't have to take them off to go to the bathroom. I'm only allowed to wear my uniform for school, so it stays nice and clean.

Mama got some of us new shoes earlier this year. Matteo Rinaldi is the shoemaker in town, and he makes us shoes out of very rough leather, and they have little tacks all over the bottom so they last longer. They certainly make a lot of noise on the cobblestones when we walk around town.

I'm not embarrassed though.

A lot of kids walk around town with noisy shoes, too.

Well there was one time I was embarrassed.

My mama would sometimes cut the fronts of the shoes out so you had room for your toes to grow.

Those are the days you feel really poor.

The rich kids got new shoes every year.

But this year was my year, and I had new shoes for the start of school.

"Paola, come on, get up, it's time to get ready for school." I command my sister. Paola and I are in the same grade, even though she is older. Mama made her stay back with me so we can share one set of books. We don't mind this, but I got really angry when Paola failed, and I had to stay back with her.

This happened twice, so I am the second oldest in class now, behind my sister.

"Ma va, Claudia, leave me alone. What's so special about school?" My sister is clearly uninterested.

"Come on Paola, don't you want to get smarter, become something?" I ask.

"Oh really, what do you think you'll ever become? We're going to get married and have babies. That's what all the women in this town do. We can live right next door to each other so our kids can play together," she says playfully.

"Nope, not me," I say with confidence. "I have plans. I want to become a teacher or a nurse, or maybe even a doctor." I am certain of it.

Paola starts laughing uncontrollably. Her belly is shaking, and her shoulders are moving up and down. I feel my face get red.

"What are you talking about, Claudia? You're crazy if you think you can ever be any of those things, especially a doctor. They're mostly men!" She says it as if I'm so stupid to think I can do this.

"Shut up, Paola. Let's just get ready for school. You need to keep up so I don't have to stay back with you again." I'm still angry at the way she laughed at me and made me feel like a fool.

"Oh, you're such a witch!" Paola says in disgust. She jumps out of bed and starts putting her uniform on. We don't usually fight, but when it comes to school, she is tough to motivate.

I braid my hair, and I can see my mother getting our basket out. Everything I do is with my sister, so we share one basket with a yellow apple, some chestnuts, and a little bread. There was some mold on it, but Mama just picks it off, hoping I won't notice.

I grab a chestnut to eat now and drink some hot coffee. Paola is just finishing her hair, so I grab the basket and pull her out the front door by the arm. My excitement is building!

"My God, Claudia, you're so wild! What's wrong with you today?" she asks, frustrated and a little breathless from having to rush to get ready.

"I just want to get to school early so we can be there when the other kids come. I want to be first," I say.

I don't like walking into a crowd once everyone else is already there and talking to each other.

As we run down our street, we bump into a few other kids who have the same idea.

"Ciao Claudia, Ciao Paola!" our classmate Angela says. She's a few years younger than us but really sharp.

"Your hair looks so pretty, Claudia, can you teach me how to braid it the way you do?" she asks.

"Sure, Angela," I say as we start walking faster toward school. "I'll show you at lunch time. It's very easy, and your hair will look so nice in a braid."

We walk the rest of the distance to school together, picking up a few other kids along the way. When we arrive, we all congregate in the courtyard, chatting about our summers, showing off our new shoes and clean uniforms, and some girls are gossiping about our teacher, Maestra Corrado.

We are on one side of the school yard, and the boys are on the other.

On the boys' side Antonio Simonelli is standing tall, a full head and shoulders above the other boys. I easily spot him in the group. He is very cute with dark wavy hair and light brown eyes. He has a strong look about him that I admire, and he's very nice. He sees me looking at him and smiles.

I think Paola likes him, so I quickly look away and walk over to the group of girls.

"I hear Maestra Corrado is going to get married," Rosa says with a funny little smirk. Everyone around gasps or giggles at the news. Rosa's eyes light up as she continues to gossip about our teacher.

"Yup, I hear she's marrying some guy she met in Naples when she visited her grandmother. It seems to be moving pretty fast." Rosa is proud of herself at what she's suggesting.

The bell rings and it's time for us to move into our classrooms.

"Oh, stop yourself, Rosa! You don't know anything about Maestra Corrado." I try to shift the attention; I don't like gossip. It makes me feel uncomfortable.

"Shush, Claudia!" Rosa waves her hand in my face. "I know more than you do, and besides, I'm not saying anything mean. I'm just thinking she may not be here for very long. You know marrying a man from Naples, she might just move there. I'm sure he's not going to want to move here," she says smugly.

We all walk inside single file, and I think about what Rosa just said. She's right. If Maestra Corrado is marrying a man from Naples, there's no way she'll be here very long.

The thought of that makes me sick to my stomach.

She's the one person in this town who always makes me feel smart, and the thought of losing her to Naples makes this place seem even more grim.

CHAPTER 3

———

It's so hot!

It's not usually this hot once we get back into school, but today I'm sweaty and sticky and I can't take it.

I'm tired of thinking about the work I have to do, and the heat is making me feel even more tired.

I need to get into some cool water fast.

Paola and I are sweeping the alley near our home before we have to walk down for the water. Then we have pasta to make and clothes to wash. And I want to spend some time on my schoolwork, too. But tomorrow is Sunday, and I can do it then.

"Paola, come here," I say, my shoulders shrugging up as I motion to her with a backward wave of my hand.

"What?" she asks as she comes over, panting and sweaty.

"Let's sneak away for a little bit, maybe go for a swim?" I say quietly.

I try to coax her with swimming since the boys are usually there, and Paola likes the attention.

"We can't! Mama will kill us if we don't get our work done," Paola says just as quietly.

"Oh, come on," I say. "I can't stand this heat anymore, and besides, Mama isn't paying attention. We can go for a quick swim, and she won't even know. Besides, Antonio might be there," I say teasingly.

I see Antonio at school all the time. I can't help but notice him since he's much cuter than the other boys in school. At lunch he likes to hang around with the girls and talk about stories we hear from our parents. He appreciates things like music and reading, not like typical boys our age. Most boys in my town want to play soccer and work with their hands. He's definitely a thinker, and I like that, and so does my sister.

"I'm not going to get in trouble because you want to be stupid and selfish," Paola states very proudly.

But I can hear in her voice that she's questioning her position.

"Come on, I know you want to. Stop fighting me, and let's go!" I say quickly, trying to persuade her.

Paola's eyes squint, and her lips purse to one side. With a dramatic toss, she sends the broom against the wall.

"Okay!" she says wholeheartedly, and we both take off running. I can already imagine how great it will be to hit the water, even if it's only for a little bit.

As we run through the town we see Mrs. Grasso, a big woman with a permanent scowl on her face. We try to hide from her since she's a big mouth and might tell our mother, but she sees us before we can get away.

"Buon giorno, Signora Grasso," we say in unison.

"What are you girls doing? You have work to do. I don't think your mother would be so happy to see you acting like *farfalle impazziti*," she says meanly. I never understood what a crazy butterfly actually did to make people think she was crazy, but I guess that's what we were acting like.

"Just walking around town to get some air before we do our work, Signora. We have lots of chores to do so we can't take too long. We'll see you later. Ciao!" we say as Mrs. Grasso shakes her head in disapproval, and we run off giggling.

We get to the bottom of town and run into a bunch of kids throwing stones in the street and playing a game. They are laughing and screaming, but we only have the cool water on our minds. Time is limited, so we just wave quickly and continue running. We come around to the bread ovens, walk to the end of the cobblestones, and start heading on to the dirt roads that lead to the pond.

Paola is humming away, making small talk and skipping down the dirt road. Out of the blue she says, "Do you think Antonio is cute?" This is a strange question since she likes him, and she knows that I know she likes him. Can she read my mind? I mean, of course I think he's cute, but my sister likes him and he's just a friend.

"Sure I think he's cute," I say. "Everyone thinks he's cute. He's probably the cutest boy in town!" I remind her.

"Yes," Paola says. "That's true, I guess, but if you are interested in him you should talk to him. I don't think he even notices me." She kicks the dirt up all over her shoes and socks.

"Why do you think that, Paola?" I ask.

"He always looks your way," she says with no emotion. "I don't know why I think that, maybe it's the way he acts when you're around."

Just at that moment, we round the curve in the road. It opens up to a big field of grain that's waiting for the last cut of the year. The pond appears just beyond the field, and the water is glistening in the early day sun. An enormous oak tree with an amazing display of branches that stretch out over top of the water grows next to the pond. It isn't a very big pond, but big enough for a group of us to enjoy on a hot day. And of course, other kids from town are already there.

I see a couple of my friends from school and some kids who graduated already whom I don't know very well. Everyone is jumping off of the tree limbs and into the pond. It is the most fun that we ever have in the warm months. A couple of boys are hanging on the tree, waiting for their turn to jump in.

"Come on," they heckle to each other. "Hurry up and get out of the way so I can jump in."

One after another they climb the tree, wait on the edge of the limb until it's clear below, and then dive into the water, hands first, making a huge splash. They come up with their hands in the air as if to say, "I'm here!"

I'm getting excited just watching them.

I kick off my shoes and socks, run to the tree, and get in line for my turn. Paola isn't in as much of a hurry as I am, so she decides to sit it out and watch with some of the boys we know from school. Three kids are ahead of me, and as each one climbs and jumps, the crowd on the side cheers and laughs.

I climb up, one branch at a time, careful not to slip. I get to the highest branch I can, shimmy to the end of it, and try my best to jump off gracefully while I twist and turn in the air. I land in the water on my back!

Antonio is on the side watching, and as I come up, I feel my face getting hot and red. I hate that he saw me mess up that jump. He runs over to the edge of the pond.

"Claudia, are you okay?" He sounds worried as he helps me out of the pond. My back stings and I feel really stupid, but I say coolly, "Sure Antonio, I'm fine!"

He helps me out of the water by grabbing my hand and pulling me up on the bank. My embarrassment disappears with this sweet, gentlemanly gesture.

"Okay, if you say so," he says, unconvinced.

We walk up to the group, and one by one, overlapping each other's comments, they ask if I'm okay.

"Sure, it wasn't that bad. I just looked stupid, but it's okay," I say humbly, and we all laugh together.

I fall onto the ground trying to conceal my pain, and Antonio sits down, too. He's already jumped a bunch of times, so he's ready for a break, and I'm happy he chose to sit down next to me.

"It's so hot today. Do you have work you have to do?" I ask, curious to know how his parents feel about him taking time away from chores for some fun.

"No, I finished all my work already. My father would beat my ass if I didn't do that first. So I got up extra early today." He speaks easily, and I feel comfortable being honest with him, too.

"We snuck away, Paola and I. My mother wasn't paying attention, so we hope we can get back before she notices." I say it with a little laugh, but I'm kind of afraid.

"Aw, it'll be okay. Even if you get caught, what's the worst that can happen?" Antonio's tone is sweet and relaxed. I enjoy his calmness; he really doesn't seem to have a care in the world.

"Ha, you don't know my mother!" I say, but I guess he's right. Maybe she would beat me with the broom or send me to bed without dinner, but I've survived those things before.

Antonio and I talk for a while, and we notice some of the kids are starting to leave. Everyone is getting tired, so we all decide to go one more time before heading back. Antonio lets me go ahead of him for my last jump. I struggle to climb up the tree and prepare to jump into the cool beautiful water, all the while thinking how much I love this pond.

"Jump, Claudia!" All the kids are watching, and Antonio is cheering me on.

As I go under, I feel like I am transported away from here, traveling to a different place. My dreams are visible in my mind, if only for a short time. I hit the bottom and push off to propel myself back up to the top as quickly as I can. As I break through the water the crowd erupts with happiness at the success of my jump.

I quickly swim out of the way to the side of the pond and climb out so I can watch Antonio do his last dive. He knows I'm watching, so he waits until I'm completely out of the water and facing him.

I drop down on the warm earth, soft grass beneath me, watching as this beautiful boy stands tall on the edge of a large branch.

He has a huge smile on his face, and he yells at the top of his lungs, "Claudia!" and then jumps.

His body seems to move in slow motion, his limbs are heavy as he lifts his arms over his head and his hands come together. He floats upward, then over and starts to point downward with his hands in prayer. It is the most spectacular dive I've ever seen, and he looks majestic!

Antonio hits the water with little splash, and just as he goes under, the pond explodes with a striking water display high up in the air. It looks like an enormous fountain, and the reality of what just happened takes my breath away.

My mouth drops open as a finger lands on the ground next to me.

CHAPTER 4

———

Kids are screaming and everyone starts running.

I feel paralyzed in the moment. I can't move or talk.

None of us know what to do or what to think.

The explosion of muddy water was all over our clothes and faces. I don't even want to think about the blood. I quickly scan the group for Paola, and I see her running toward me.

"Oh my God, Claudia, what just happened?" My sister is screaming, crying, and her face is dark with bloody mud.

"I...I...I'm not sure." I can't get any words out. "I guess it was a bomb."

"Where's Antonio? What happened to Antonio?" Paola says in disbelief and on the verge of tears.

I feel the pain of what I already know about Antonio.

"He's dead, Paola," I say, snapping out of my haze and suddenly feeling like I need to cry. The tears run down my cheeks, and I grab my sister and hug her tightly.

Minutes seem like hours, and I don't want to let her go.

"Let's go, Paola, we need to go. We have to tell Mama what happened." I pull my sister by her arm as we turn away from the pond.

Most of the other kids are already long gone, but a few are still with us, crying in the aftermath. As we run toward the town, I hear the voices of men who are running toward us. One of them yells, "What happened? We heard an explosion. What happened?"

But we can't speak.

I run frantically with my sister, past the men, and the cobblestones tell us we're almost home. We run up Corso della Vittoria and to the *Fontana* where everyone is gathering and is already hearing the news. Women are crying, trying to find Antonio's mother. The people in town are yelling at us, asking us questions, but all we want to do is get home.

We run up Via Danielle to Via Silvio Pellico. As we turn the corner and start up the alley, we see our mother at the top with a broom in her hand. For sure she's going to beat us with it but as we run up, we're crying and dirty and she stops to ask us what's wrong.

"Cosa successo, perche stai piangendo?" She drops the broom and grabs my shoulders, shaking me, asking why we're crying. The news hasn't reached her yet.

"Antonio e morto!" He's dead, I say, crying in disbelief at what I had witnessed. Paola is on the ground, sobbing.

"Oh Dio!" She takes a fast breath in, and her shoulders slump as she lets it out. My mother knows what it's like to lose a child. She brings us inside and asks us what happened. My sister sits quietly as I tell her the grim details about what we saw at the pond. She tells us to get ourselves cleaned up, and off she goes, most likely to see Antonio's mother, I can't be sure.

Paola sits at the table and stares ahead quietly.

I grab a small pail and put clean water in it from the barrel. I have two small rags, and I wet one and wipe her face. I go around her hair line, smoothing her dark wet hair back. I rinse the rag several times as I clean the dirt off her face.

Once I finish with Paola, I clean myself up. I don't care how dirty I am right now, I just need my face to be clean. I dump the dirty water outside and then go back to sit at the table in silence with my sister.

When our brothers and sisters heard the news, they all came back to the house, asking a million questions.

The last thing I want to do is talk about it. Antonio is gone. He was the sweetest boy in town, and now he's gone.

I walk over to the bed and lie down so I can get away from them. Paola was already asleep, and I just want to close my eyes and forget this ever happened. I fall asleep pretty hard and fast, and I stay that way until my mother opens the door.

I jump up, startled a bit, and ask, "Mama, where were you?" Even though I know the answer.

"I went to see Mrs. Simonelli, poor woman." She begins to tell me all about the visitors in the house and how Mrs. Simonelli was crying and falling on the floor. I can't blame her; Antonio was the best of her kids. Makes me wonder why God does things like this. Why would he let Antonio blow up? I can't seem to find the answer.

"How did she find out what happened?" I ask my mother, wondering who told her and how.

"As soon as some of the kids got back into town, they ran into Don Tommaso. He was on his way to visit a sick woman and give her Communion. The kids were crying and told him the whole story, so he went up to help find Mrs. Simonelli right away and break the news to her. She's in shock," my mother says with little emotion.

I know she's sad about it; she liked Antonio, too. And I know she's feeling bad for Mrs. Simonelli, but she's seen a lot of bad things happen.

"Mama, I'm sorry we went off the way we did this morning. Paola and I were hot and tired, and it was my idea, and I'm sorry." I just keep rattling off hoping she won't get mad and beat me with the broom.

"I can't believe you would do something like this, Claudia! You and Paola know better! *What if something happened to you*?" Her voice was getting louder and louder. "You know there are still bombs around from the war. You have to be very careful where you go. This was the dumbest thing you've ever done, and you're lucky you didn't get killed. Were you jumping, too? *What if that was you*?" She yells question after question.

For the first time, I see tears in my mother's eyes.

"Yes, Mama, we were jumping, too, but we only went a couple of times. I can't believe Antonio is gone, Mama. It was so awful. We should've never been jumping off that tree, none of us should have done it. Maybe Antonio would still be here if we didn't do it." I wonder out loud.

"Claudia, please, remember this day. Don't take crazy risks like that. Don't find yourself in places you're not supposed to be. It's an important lesson to learn, and it's good you're learning it now." Her face was sad when she said that, as if there was way more behind that comment than I knew about. But that was typical of my mother.

"I won't, Mama, I promise. I won't ever take any chances like that ever again!" I say as I hug her tightly.

And I really believe it.

CHAPTER 5

——

It's only been a few weeks since Antonio died, but the weather feels drastically different. I can feel a slight chill in the air, and the fields are starting to be scarce of food, but we go looking for greens to eat anyway.

Today Mama is coming with me instead of Paola. Ever since I saw Antonio die, I feel a softness from her that I never felt before. I'm glad she's coming.

"Mama, when are we going to the field?" I want to go and come back quickly so I can go out with my school friends later. Everyone is planning to watch Juventus play Milan on the television at the bar. I'm not really interested in soccer, but it would be fun to watch with my friends.

"Soon, Claudia. We're going to bring Lidia and Elena with us so they can help," she says as she rustles around near the fire getting things ready. I hate when my little sisters come with us. "Paola can stay home with Sophia and the boys," Mama finishes.

"Oh, Mama, why do they have to come? We can get the job done much faster if we just go ourselves. You and I could make the trip and get back fast." I plead with her so we don't waste time.

"Eh, I would like that, but they have to learn, too, Claudia. We have to teach them the things we know so they can do it for themselves someday. Come on, we're leaving soon," Mama says as she puts a couple of small knives in the basket.

"Do I have to go? I hate picking greens. I don't even like to eat them! And it's cold today," Lidia whines, stating her opinion carefully so our mother doesn't hear.

"Yes, you have to go," I say, taking a deep breath. "You have to learn how to do this like the rest of us." I say exhaling deliberately.

"Okay, Claudia, but can you braid my hair? I don't want to get any bugs in it." Lidia asks sweetly. Of course, I do it. Braiding her hair is something I always do. Like washing her clothes and helping her dress and teaching her all kinds of girl responsibilities. I resent it.

"Ow, Claudia, stop being so rough!" she cries.

"Oh, come on Lidia, you're such a baby. And just because you don't like greens doesn't mean you're not going." I finish braiding her hair and tie off the end.

"Come on, put on your field clothes and let's get moving." I say with urgency.

I spend a lot of time taking care of my siblings. There's so many of them, and my mother can't always do it. The toughest days are when she goes to work cleaning the post office. She doesn't work a lot of hours there, but she works enough to need extra help from me. Between that and getting food, and taking care of the smallest children, it doesn't leave her time for the rest of us.

After I finish with Lidia, I tell her to go wait near the door so I can help Elena.

Elena is younger, not very sweet, but not at a point in her life where she's questioning very much. Her hair is too short to braid so I quickly tie it up in a ponytail as Mama comes to the door.

"Andiamo!" she says hopefully, and we follow like little bees following the queen. We walk down our alley to the main street, and off we go down the hill. The streets are full of people. There's a buzz about town in anticipation of the soccer game that brings everyone outside. We greet all the people we pass, but we don't dare stop to chat. We have a job to do, and Mama is on a mission.

The sun is shining, and it helps calm the chill I feel in my bones. The Fontana is glistening, and the red brick stripes are so bright and inviting. People are always there getting water, it seems, and today is no different. I hear the refreshing sound of water splashing into the buckets as we walk by.

We proceed down to the bottom of town and start our trek on the dirt roads away from Orsara. It isn't that far, maybe a forty-minute walk, but it's hard for the girls to keep up.

"I'm thirsty," says Elena, with her little ponytail swaying back and forth. She's very slight, so she can't handle much activity.

"Why didn't you get some water when we passed the fountain? Now you have to wait until we get to the field. It's not much farther and you can get a little drink in the nearby creek when we arrive," I say, trying to soothe her.

We continue walking and chatting with each other about the past. Conversations that start with, "Do you remember this?" or "Do you remember that?" Elena doesn't remember much, but Lidia has a better memory, and of course my mother has a lot to say.

"I used to walk through this area all the time when I was young." My mother seems happy talking about her childhood. "We had to go to the fields to get food just like we're doing now," she says almost with a little pride.

I think about what she just said and how sad it is. She used to do this when she was young, and here she is with her own children still doing it. I don't know where I'll be when I'm her age, but I hope it isn't walking to these fields to pick greens with my kids.

"Mama, I don't want to live in Orsara when I'm older," I say, cringing with anticipation at my mother's response, but this seemed like a good time to bring it up.

"What do you mean, you don't want to live here? Where you gonna go?" she asks as her shoulders rise up and in toward her chest.

"I'm not sure, Mama, but I want to go to school, a big school. Not like the one we have here. I want to learn to be a teacher or a nurse maybe." I don't say doctor this time. Paola made me feel foolish for that.

"Claudia, don't fill your head with crazy ideas. We have our family here and plenty to do. You can get a job here as soon as you're done with school," she says as she grabs Elena's hand to pull her along.

"Maybe working with the seamstress would be good for you. You're good at sewing. You took all those lessons after school so you can put that skill to good use," she offers.

"But Mama, I don't want to stay here and sew. I want to go to a big school." I was getting frustrated.

I want my mother to listen to what I'm saying, but I can tell she's not interested in discussing it.

"Well let's not waste time talking about it now. Girls, come on, move faster!"

She changes the subject by bellowing at us to pick up the pace.

I keep my annoyance and disappointment to myself. I feel like what I want to do seems impossible to her, anyway. We keep walking, kicking rocks, the dust from the road turning my black shoes gray. We get to the field, and my mother pulls out the little knives. She starts by clipping the greens at the end near the ground, showing my sisters as she does it. She scrapes the ends with her knife before she hands them over to the girls to put in the basket I'm holding.

I'm bored like you can't even imagine and, then across the field I see someone. He's tall and he's wearing a cap. He looks to be older than me from what I can see.

We continue cutting greens, and it seems we're getting closer and closer. He's coming more into focus, and I can make out his features.

"Ciao!" he says in a friendly voice.

My mother says nothing and just looks at him curiously. She's not overly friendly with anyone.

I answer politely, "Ciao," with a smile I can't control.

"It's a beautiful day out here to pick some old greens. They're tough, but the animals seem to like them," he says.

My mother looks at him with a cold stare, and I can see she wishes he hadn't said that.

"Yes, they are," I say, wanting to get off the subject quickly. Before I can think of anything else to say, he begins to walk away.

"Good day." He tips his hat and flashes a smile that I get lost in.

"Wait, what's your name?" I ask, feeling my mother's angry glare in the back of my head.

"Marcello. Piacere!" he says as he turns with the basket of greens for his animals and walks away.

I was intrigued by this boy who was picking greens like us, and from that point on I couldn't think of anything else. I started to imagine what his life must be like on the farm.

Does he ever leave his farm? Maybe go to a big town, like Milan? I wonder if he thinks about getting away from here like I do. Maybe get married and have a family and live in a big city. My imagination was wild with possibilities.

"Claudia, come on, keep moving. We're almost done. And stop acting like a little puttana," Mama says with a disgusted tone. I hate when she uses that word.

We finish the job and start to walk off. I think about Marcello the entire way home. The girls were skipping around and happy to be going back. Mama was on a mission to get home and start cooking.

When will I see him again?

I'll have to come back to this field again soon.

Marcello Field. That's what I'll call it.

On the walk home I smell the sweet, acidic smell of grapes fermenting into wine. The fruit stand has persimmons that are bright orange and look to be delicious, but we don't stop. I can only imagine what it would be like to take a bite out of that decadent fruit, sure to be full of flavor.

I feel my hunger taking control of my mind again.

We walk up the street to our alley and turn onto Via Silvio Pellico. It's October and cool in the close quarters of our street. It's a typical day, with clothes hanging on lines, people hanging off their second stories, and some people sitting in chairs outside.

We get back to the house and start cooking. I feel upset about what my mother said to me in the field. I know she doesn't value school the way I do, and it's because we're poor. School is a dream that rich kids can follow, but not us.

She didn't get very far in school, and all she did was have babies every year. I knew I didn't want to do that, so I brought it up again.

"Mama, I want to talk about school. I want to get my degree from a bigger school than what we have in Orsara. I don't want to stay in this town." My voice is cracking, and I can feel my face getting hot again.

"Claudia, you can't go to school in another town. You know we don't have money for that. Besides, you want too much. You're filling your head with these ideas that can't happen," she says as she gets more annoyed with me, but I see something different there. A look on her face that makes me feel like she probably wished for more than she got, too. A look that says she wanted more out of life than living here and having babies. A look that tells me I have to fight for what I want, no matter how hard it is or how much resistance I get.

I back down a little. I think after seeing that look on her face, maybe now isn't a good time to push, so I let it go. We have to make dinner, anyway.

"I'll go get the boys rounded up for dinner." I walk out the door and start up the alley. All the kids like to hang in an open area up around the corner, and that's exactly where I find my brothers, kicking the soccer ball around with some friends. "Let's go, it's almost time for dinner," I order.

—————

That night, Paola and I go to town with friends to watch the soccer game. As soon as I get there, I can't help but notice this handsome boy, and he's walking to me. It's Marcello!

"Ciao Signorina," he says very politely. He's cleaned up since I saw him in the field earlier. "I was hoping I'd see you here tonight to watch the game. What's your name, anyway?"

"Claudia Valentino." I reach my hand out to shake his.

"Pleasure to meet you again, Claudia Valentino. And it's going to be a good one tonight. I want Juventus to win, how about you?" he asks excitedly.

I don't really care who wins so I agree with him, "Sure, Juventus!"

"Do you know anything about these teams?" he asks, sensing that I don't.

Giggling, I say, honestly, "No, not really. I just wanted to come out to town tonight, so I told my mother I was coming to watch the game with my friends from school."

"How much do *you* know about these teams?" I ask teasingly.

"Well, I know a lot about the teams actually. Juventus has a great record and is favored to win. They have Boniperti. He's the best!" Marcello continues on about soccer. I'm not really interested in sports, but I like listening to the enthusiasm in his voice when he talks about it.

"Do you like to play soccer, too?" I ask, trying to make conversation.

"I used to," he says right away. Then he thinks a little more and tells me why he doesn't play anymore.

"I have too much work to do on my parent's farm. It's my job now. My dad's not able to do as much as he used to, so I had to take over for him as soon as I finished school. Doesn't leave me with much time for fun." He lets out a deep breath and his shoulders drop. "But it's okay." He resolves in his mind.

"Well, what would you do if you could do anything?" I ask, really curious to hear about his dreams.

"Honestly, I would like to be in the navy. I always thought it would be cool to work on a submarine, you know, underwater?" Marcello clarified.

"I know what a submarine is," I say quickly. Did he really think I didn't know?

"I can tell you for sure I wouldn't want to be under water. I like being in the water, but not completely underneath like that. No way." I am adamant in my statement, terrified at the thought of it.

"Well, it's definitely something I would like to do, but my parents won't let me leave town. If I'm not here to help with the farm, no one will be, and I can't do that to them." Marcello says with a little sadness in his voice.

What he just said hit me hard and I feel bad for him. There's nothing I dream about more than leaving this town and finding new and exciting things to do in life. I see Marcello's life already playing out in my mind. The next fifty years have already been decided for him by his parents.

I realize that he's stuck here, and I think he realizes it, too.

Suddenly the crowd around the bar erupts, and we remember we're here to watch a game.

"Come on, Marcello," I say encouragingly, "let's go over and watch the game. It sounds like it's getting good!"

———————

The game last night was exciting, and Juventus beat Milan three to one. Everyone loved it, including Marcello.

Sunday morning, I'm groggy and caught between being awake and in a lovely little dream. I'm running in a field of beautiful flowers; it's a sunny day and I'm wearing a baby blue dress with a white collar. I feel so peaceful and relaxed that I don't want to wake up and leave this beautiful place. I don't know where I am running to, but it feels good and I feel free.

My stomach is grumbling, and I have no idea what time it is.

The house is dark and the window on the door is covered.

No one is moving in the house, and it feels strange.

Usually, our home has some activity, my mother telling me to do something, go get water or start the day's chores, but not today. I fall back to sleep and I'm lucky enough to continue my dream. The flowers, all different colors, are swaying in the light breeze. Beautiful rainbows of red, pink, yellow, and white. Brilliant green leaves and stems, and off in the distance on one side was a dark wooded area. Straight ahead was open sky...and that's where I go.

What a lovely feeling to have no barriers in front of you.

I feel it deep in my body, what it must be like to have the freedom to go wherever you want.

Suddenly, we hear a knock on the door. My mother rustles around and goes to the door quickly. She cracks it open slightly, and I see bright daylight coming through. I can't imagine how late it is. Given the way the light was coming in, it's probably close to lunch.

It is a nun from our church

"Buon giorno, Signora Valentino," Sister says.

"Buon giorno," says my mother reluctantly.

"We didn't see any of your family at church this morning, and we were worried. Is everything okay?"

"Yes, of course we are all okay. The children are just tired and have been working very hard, so I wanted to let them sleep," my mother explains. I know the real reason she keeps us in. She doesn't want to admit it to Sister.

"We can bring you some things to help out. Maybe some flour or beans? God is always with us and wants to take care of his children," Sister says in a loving and understanding way.

She knows my mother doesn't like to take handouts, but she could only keep the troops under control for so long. Eventually empty bellies would start complaining.

"No, Sister," my mother whispers, "we are okay, but grazie!" She closes the door tightly, adjusting the curtain to shut out the light again.

I feel so mad at my mother then, but also conflicted. My stomach is empty, and we have a houseful of children, so why not accept something from the church? But the conflicted part of me understands. The shame and embarrassment are too much to bear. Everyone in the town would know. Everyone would see that we accepted food. It was almost worth having an empty stomach. Almost.

I stay in bed so I don't have to face my mother. I know it's a bad time for our family once again. So I keep my mouth shut and face the wall so she can't see me. I try to fall back to sleep and get back into that beautiful dream, but this time it's not working. My mind is racing, and the dream is long gone. Somehow, I manage to fall asleep again, and this time I don't dream.

I don't know how much time passes, but then I hear another knock on the door. This time when my mother cracks it open, a little less light comes in.

And sitting right outside our door was food!

Pasta, a loaf of bread, cheese, beans, and even flour so we could make whatever we wanted.

All just appeared on this beaten-up, old wooden cart.

There's enough food for all of us for a few days at least, although I know we can stretch it much longer than that. My mother's shoulders drop, she lets out a very deep breath, and quickly brings the cart inside. She looks up and down our street before closing the door behind her.

The street is empty, and it's like this amazing cart of food just appeared out of nowhere.

"Mama, where did that come from?" I ask.

"It's a beautiful gift from the angels. They know we're struggling right now, and they sent it to us," Mama says with relief in her voice.

Immediately she let some light into our very dark and dreary home, and life started to awaken. The kids open their eyes and stretch their arms high in the air. We all gather around our table and enjoy a little bread and cheese, just enough food to satisfy us for the day. We could easily devour it all immediately, but my mother is too careful for that kind of reckless behavior.

She has to make that food stretch for a few days, until Papa gets home and we can buy some things we need.

It's a beautiful meal, and everyone feels good.

Except my mother.

Deep down inside, she knows that the food came from Sister, and she hates to be dependent on anyone or anything.

CHAPTER 6

Ice is forming on the cobblestones when we throw out dirty water, and I can see my breath. It's almost Christmastime, and my favorite time of the year!

My father is home now for a stretch. When the weather starts to change, he stays close to home. His last job got us enough money to hold us over for a little while, and he always has little odd jobs so we get by.

Our pig is gone, so now we have meat for winter. We keep it under salt in a wooden bin built into the floor so it doesn't spoil. My mother trades some of the meat for other food so it feels like we have plenty to eat these days.

We get packages from America full of goodies for our whole family around this time of year, too. They come from my Zia Lucia, who is my father's half sister and lives in Gary, Indiana. I know nothing about Indiana except that it is in America so Zia Lucia must be rich. She prepares these great packages that we get around three times a year, and the best packages are at Christmas.

Clothes that are new to us, chocolates, chewing gum, canned milk—things that make us feel special.

"Go to the post office, Claudia," says my mother. "They have some packages for us. And bring your brothers to help you."

"Okay, Mama," I say excitedly. "I'll go now!" Of course, I can't wait a minute longer to get out the door.

"Dominic, Giorgio," I yell from the doorway, "come here now." I wait to hear some noise, but nothing.

"Dominic, Giorgio," I yell, stretching out their names as I get louder this time, and more impatient.

"Dominic..." Finally I hear the echoing of their feet hitting the cobblestones around the corner.

"We're coming!" they say in frustration as they run closer and their footsteps get louder.

"Claudia, what do you want?" asks Dominic, the older of the two boys.

"We have to go to the post office to get our packages from America. Let's go now!"

I grab a shawl to wrap over my dress, and we go, the three of us, walking down the alley of Via Silvio Pellico to Via Roma. We turn left and walk uphill to the post office. It's about a ten-minute walk from our house, and luckily a mild day to be outside.

My palms are starting to itch; I feel so excited of what's to come!

We get to the post office and find four packages there. Big boxes wrapped in brown paper and tied with thin white string. Addressed to my mother.

"Dominic, you take the biggest package, Giorgio take the next largest, and I'll carry the other two." I grab the packages as I tell them what to do.

"Okay." They're just as happy as I am about the packages, and they know better than to argue with me right now.

We start back down Via Roma toward our house. It's an easy walk, but when you're carrying heavy packages, it's a little trickier. The cobblestones are hard to navigate, and the steps along the way even more so. I'm trying to avoid the ice patches, so it looks like I'm dancing and skipping around. As we get to the bottom of our street, Lidia and Elena come running toward us. Their footsteps are loud as they run to grab a box.

My two little sisters take the largest, holding either end of the box, balancing it carefully to get it home. They're just as excited as we are!

"Giorgio, Dominic," I scream, "come on, move faster!" I know as soon as my sisters get to the house the box will be ripped open, and I don't want to miss out on anything.

I hand Dominic one of my boxes, and at once the three of us start running up the street after the girls. We get to the house and put them on the floor so my mother can open them. She grabs a small knife to cut the string and then she lets the youngest ones rip the paper off.

In an instant, all three boxes are unwrapped of the brown paper, opened, and cloth is visible on top.

"What's inside? Let's see!" I say with excitement. The younger kids are squealing with delight in anticipation of what goodies there will be in the boxes, and this delivery does not disappoint. As soon as my mother removes the cloth from the first box, we see chocolate Hershey bars, Dentyne cinnamon chewing gum, and cans of Carnation milk; plenty of treats for all of us to enjoy, and everyone is grinning from ear to ear. I can smell the sweetness coming out of the boxes and filling up our little kitchen.

As my mother continues to go through the boxes, she uncovers small writing booklets and pencils. I get excited and ask for one for myself. I need somewhere to write my dreams, to make my plans, and a little booklet is just the thing. I put them aside so I can pay attention to what else is in the boxes.

Sweaters for the younger kids, long pants for the boys, and dresses for my older sister and me, which are all used but in great condition. They don't fit us perfectly, but they are close enough and we feel happy.

At the bottom of one box is a pair of rubber boots, short ones that you put over your shoes. I see those and know they will fit me so I grab them as quickly as I can.

Now my socks and shoes won't get wet when I walk through puddles in town. I put them on instantly and walk around the house to show them off.

"Mama, there are some nice things in here, don't you think?" I say happily as I point my foot and twist it around for my mother to see. I wonder if she'd like anything in there for herself.

"Of course I'm happy. We are so lucky to have family who cares about us, and I'm always grateful for anything they send," says my mother, and she looks happy. She looks really happy. Maybe she's excited for all of us.

"What about you, Claudia? Are you happy with anything in particular?" She smirks. She knows I love the boots.

"Yes, Mama, the boots are great!" I exclaim and rush over to hug her. Hugging my mother is not something I usually do, but I feel so joyful and have to show it.

"Well that's good. You can share them with Paola," my mother says. I ignore her since nothing is going to squash the happiness I'm feeling right now. These boots make me feel on top of the world, and I can't wait to wear them out in town tomorrow.

We have a great night, trying on the clothes and eating some of the goodies, but not all of them. We have to save some for Christmas. My mother takes the goodies and puts them in the cabinet near the kitchen table where we keep our food. Everyone knows not to touch it.

We go to bed that night feeling happy and full, which are feelings we don't often have.

And tomorrow, I can't wait to wear my new boots.

———————

I wake up to a little light coming in through our door near the front of the house. I know what time it is as soon as I open my eyes, and so I get out of bed a little more quickly than usual. I'm so excited to get the water today, since I get to wear my new boots. I jump out of bed and put on a brown shirt and skirt and braid my hair.

The fire is crackling, and a strong smell of coffee is filling the room. Mama is working a cleaning shift at the post office, which she has to get done before they open for the day. My father is sitting at the table alone with his back to me.

"Good morning, Papa, what are you doing?" I sit next to him so we can talk a little. I don't get a lot of time with father alone, and I want it today.

"Rolling cigarettes," he states with no feeling. He's very focused.

As soon as I sit down, the fragrant scent of tobacco mixes with the smell of the coffee, and I see a small tin with rolling papers on the table.

"It's cold out today," he says. He knows I'm about to go out, so that's his way of telling me to dress warmly. But right now, I am intrigued by what he's doing.

"Papa, wouldn't it be easier to just buy cigarettes? This way is so messy." I start sweeping the fallen tobacco with my hand, into a little pile.

"Probably," he says, "but it saves money, and I like doing it. I can make the cigarettes any size I want." He holds one up that he just rolled, showing me his work. The white paper is wrapped perfectly into a chubby cigarette with twisted ends.

That makes sense to me. We are always looking for ways to save money. I notice the pot of coffee on the fire bubbling up. It is a speckled metal-looking thing that we use every day. I love the sweet smell of coffee, even though I don't love the bitter taste.

"Come on, go get water, your mother will be back from work soon," he says.

The light is shining in, and the others are starting to wake up. I put my new boots on over my shoes and wrap my shawl around me. I find a rag from the kitchen, roll it up, and put it on my head before placing the barrel on top. The barrel has metal handles on the sides that I have to hold on to in order to keep it balanced on my head. Some people are very accomplished in balancing the barrel and don't use their hands at all! Not me though; I need to hold on.

I walk outside and can see that everyone is already up and out, starting the day's activities.

"Buon giorno, Signora Ferrara, how are you today?"

"Eh, my bones hurt and it's cold out. I'm getting older every day. La vecchiaia!" she says in a tone that tells me she hates old age.

"Well, that's better than the alternative, right?" I say jokingly. Knowing full well that she's pretty close to the alternative already. She waves an annoyed hand, shooing me away.

I get closer to town, and the morning buzz echoes against the buildings. People are talking about the weather, and I hear someone predict a very cold winter ahead. I turn the corner, and a long line of people are waiting at the Fontana.

"Buon giorno," a young man in line says. It's Tonino. He's a few years older than me, and I know him from town, but I don't really know him that well. We both have the job of getting water in our houses, so I see him here often.

"Buon giorno, Tonino. How's your mother doing?" She's been sick for a while and it seemed like she might not make it, but somehow she's still around.

"She's good, thank you," he says with an exasperated tone. "She feels good enough to get up and cook for us, but she can't do much else. But she's okay." He offers up a little more information than is usual, since no one ever likes to talk about their family around here. We keep it in, never share too much.

We talk a little about nothing special as I try to draw attention to my feet. How could he not notice my boots? I sit on the ledge and swing my feet left and right. Finally, he notices.

"Hey those are cool shoes," he says. "Where did you get them?"

"My father's family in America sent them over for me." I stretch the truth a little. "You can't get anything like these here," I say proudly. I want everyone to see my new boots.

"Yes, they are very nice," Tonino says as he moves to the Fontana. He is next in line. The water splashes all around until he positions the barrel just right under the steady stream as it begins to fill. He taps his fingers against the wood and whistles a little as he waits. Before long he grabs the barrel and puts it on top of his head.

He walks away, calling back to me, "Have a good day, Claudia, see you next time."

"Ciao Tonino," I say as I walk up to take my turn at the Fontana. As it fills up, I look around at the town center. People smoking and having an espresso in the small bar across the street, the sun shining on a little patch of ice along the side of the road. It feels brighter than usual.

A peaceful calm fills town; it feels good, and once the water barrel is overflowing, I plug it up and put it back on my head. It isn't a very far walk, thank God, since the barrel is pretty heavy once it's full.

I walk up the streets and hear the little tune in my head that Tonino was whistling. It's a happy one, and I feel a smile creeping up on my face.

When I turn onto my street, I feel the barrel start to slip, so I quickly adjust. As I straighten it and try to get my balance back, I step on a patch of ice.

I feel myself losing control.

I dance around trying to save myself from falling but can't do it. The barrel slips off my head and the metal handle goes down onto the cobblestones with a bang, my pinky finger underneath it.

The pain is unbearable, and I see stars. I hear myself screaming almost as if it's someone else. It's so loud that everyone comes running!

"Aaaaahhhhhhhhhhh." I drop the barrel to the ground. It rolls down the street a few feet, hits a house, and pops open. All the water rushes down the street, and I can't stop crying.

"Aaaahhhh." The pain takes my breath away, and I hold my hand up in the air as blood runs down my arm.

"Oh Jesu, Claudia, what happened?" Signora Ferrara asks.

"I slipped on the ice, and the barrel went down on my finger. Please get my father." But just as I say that, my brother is running down the alley with my father right behind him.

My brother tries to help me, but there is nothing he can do. My father takes his outer vest off to wrap my hand and stop the bleeding, and he helps me up off the ground.

"Claudia, can you walk? Come on, get up, and let's go to the *Farmacia*," my father says with concern. The pharmacy is the only place in town that might be able to help.

But as I start to get up, my legs get wobbly, and I can't move.

I feel like I'm going to pass out from the pain, and blood is everywhere. My father picks me up and carries me down to the Farmacia near the fountain.

"Claudia, what did you do to yourself?" the pharmacist asks as he starts to unwrap the vest around my finger. I am bleeding all over his shop, and I don't think he is too happy about it.

"I slipped on the ice, and the water barrel fell on my finger," I say through the tears.

"Well," he says, "serves you right, wearing those boots around town in this weather. Don't you know they're for the springtime, for puddles, not ice?" he says.

He holds pressure on my now-distorted finger until the bleeding slows, then he washes it off with water.

Once he does that, I can see my finger is hooked inward and doesn't look normal at all. I start crying again from the sight of it.

He then disinfects it and wraps it up with some gauze and sends us on our way. He hands my father his bloody vest and tells me to get some rest as we walk out. All the towns-people are gathered around wondering what the excitement is all about.

"She's okay," my father says with confidence enough for both of us. "She's better now, and we're going home." I try not to cry in front of everyone. I want to look strong and smart, especially since I feel dumb for wearing those shoes. I just want to get home and take them off. I didn't know they were for spring.

We walk up the street, and the pain is almost unbearable, but I try not to think about it. As we get close, I notice the water barrel is gone, and when we get to the house, I see it sitting by the front door. I guess one of my brothers brought it back.

My mother comes over to me, takes a quick look at my hand, and I can see the look of disappointment in her face. We both know what it means if I can't use my hand.

"Are you okay? Does it hurt?" Mama looks concerned.

"I'm okay, Mama," I say quietly, but I feel like I'm going to die from the pain.

"Okay, let's sit down to eat something," she says since she has prepared some food already. It's midmorning so we have a little bread and milk to satisfy us until dinner.

After I eat a little, I feel nauseous, so I go to lie down. As soon as I get to my bed, I turn around and throw up on the floor.

"I'm sorry, Mama." I feel so sick but feel even worse for throwing up my food.

"It's, okay, Claudia, lie down and try to relax. You probably have indigestion."

I lie in bed and start to cry; the pain is overwhelming.

CHAPTER 7

———

I was crying all night.

I wake up after a horrible night of pain, and my father says we're going to the hospital.

"Claudia, let's go. You need to see a doctor." My mother helps me up and wraps a shawl around my shoulders.

"Okay," I say with a whimper, exhausted and still crying from the pain.

"I'm sorry you're hurting," Paola says affectionately. "Don't worry, I'll take care of your chores." She smiles halfheartedly. All the other kids are watching us quietly.

We have an old scooter, a Lambretta, that we use only in an emergency since gas is expensive. I wait with my mother as my father goes around to a back alley where he keeps it parked. It is light army green and rusted in a lot of spots.

"Hop on, Claudia," my father says hurriedly.

My mother helps me get on the back of the scooter, and I try to hold on with one hand as best I can. She smooths my hair back from my forehead, and her touch comforts me. I can tell Papa is worried and in a hurry, and not very sensitive to the fact that I can barely hold on. He starts off quickly and I almost fall off, but he slows a bit and I catch my balance. We set off for the hospital in Foggia, a good forty kilometers away.

The roads to Foggia are bumpy and dusty, and the cold wind is going right through me. We have no protection from the weather on this scooter, and our clothes are not very warm. I cry into my father's back, trying to muffle the sound.

I can feel my father's tension building.

I can tell it bothers him to hear me cry.

He drives faster and faster with every squeeze of my good hand around his chest.

When we arrive at Ospedali Riuniti di Foggia, we find nurses in stiff, white aprons and caps all around. The doctors are smart-looking men with cigarettes in their hands. As soon as we walk in the door, one of the nurses comes to help me. I'm crying and the blood has soaked through the gauze from the day before.

"Oh, child what happened to you?" says this very pretty nurse who looks about the same age as my teacher.

"A water barrel fell onto my finger, and I think it's broken," I say, not knowing how else to explain my injury.

My father adds, "It happened yesterday. We took her to the town doctor, and he wrapped it up like this. But she was crying all night."

The nurse brings us inside and quickly unravels the gauze. Her face twists as she looks at my distorted hand. It's like her face took on the shape of it. I forget about the pain for a split second and feel myself getting more upset because of her reaction. It really looks bad, and suddenly I worry about what is going to happen to my hand in this hospital. I grab my father's arm tightly with my good hand, and I can see that he looks worried, too.

The nurse calls the doctor in, and he takes a look at my hand. He is tall with dark hair and blue eyes, possibly the most beautiful man I have ever seen. Somehow the pain just manages to drift away, for a second. Dr. Blue Eyes holds my hand up gently to take a closer look.

Dr. Blue Eyes and Nurse Twisted Face talk to each other about my hand, and I understand there isn't much they can do.

"We're going to clean this mess up. Nurse, please bring me the tray. I'll need some fresh gauze and ointment from the draw," Dr Blue Eyes instructs the nurse.

"Of course, Doctor," Nurse Twisted Face says without hesitation.

"And please go prepare a bed for Signor..." The doctor fumbles a bit over what to say.

"What's your name?" he asks in a caring voice. Suddenly I relax a bit.

"Claudia Valentino," I say quietly, finding it difficult to speak with the fear that's now building up inside.

"Okay, Ms. Valentino, we're going to put a cast on your arm so your hand can heal in the correct position. Do you know what that is?" He gathers together the supplies the nurse brought over and starts laying them out on the tray.

I have seen casts on kids in the past, so I answer very smartly "Yes, of course I know." Although I don't really know exactly how the doctors make them. I assume he knows what he's doing, though. "Is it going to hurt?" I ask cringing, hoping he says no.

"Well only a little when I adjust your finger. But you look like a strong girl, you'll be okay." His voice is calm as he cleans my bloody hand and looks more closely at my mangled finger.

Nurse Twisted Face and Dr. Blue Eyes start working. They clean my wrist and hand of all the dried blood with some cotton that is wet, and it stings a little. I pull my arm back slightly and wince.

"I'm sorry if that hurts, it'll just be a little longer," he says, cleaning my arm more gently. I bite my lip to ease the pain and soon he is finished with cleaning off the wound. He takes a quick look and tries to manipulate my finger to a straight position as I scream out loud. I can taste the saltiness of my tears as they run down my cheeks and into my mouth.

He then begins casting it all the way up my arm, in a slightly bent position. He leaves just a little square opening near the wound that looks like a window.

"What's that for?" I ask curiously.

"It's so we can easily administer medicine to prevent infection," he says as he continues smoothing the layers of my wet cast.

The nurse goes to prepare my bed. I'm in a lot of pain and it's all I can think about. I say goodbye to my father, who then goes to talk to a different nurse at the desk outside of my room. I start to move and feel queasiness take over. The nurse quickly brings over a wheelchair and then pushes me down the white hallway to a set of double doors. Inside are rows and rows of metal beds with clean, white sheets and fluffy pillows, and I start to feel lucky. I have never slept in an actual bed with a mattress, alone, without my brothers and sisters around.

This is all new to me.

She wheels me down the hall, and as we pass each of the beds, I can see different patients; some look sick, and some don't. We get close to the end of the row, which has one empty bed, second to last.

The nurse walks over to pull the sheets down before helping me up and walking me toward the bed gently, knowing that the pain was making me feel really sick. I lie down under the sheets, rest my head on the pillow, and immediately feel better.

I close my eyes and quickly fall into a state of partial sleep, dreaming about cool, blue water. I am swimming underwater where it is quiet and peaceful. I can see fish swimming around, and I can even make out the bottom of the sea.

Suddenly I hear some banging noises. My eyes are still closed, and I don't know where I am. I can't bring myself to open my eyes yet, so I just lie there and listen to the noise.

Nurses talking, metal clanging, wheels turning.

I flutter my eyes a bit and see some blurry images. Nurses are walking down the aisles, pushing carts. The smell of food fills the room, and my stomach starts to grumble.

"Come on, get up," one of the nurses says, and it echoes into the high ceiling of the large room. "Ora di mangiare," says one of the nurses. "It's time to eat," she says again as I sit up in anticipation of something delicious.

"Do we really have to eat now?" asks a girl next to me.

She has short, dark hair that I envy. I would love to cut my hair short, but my mother won't let me. And why is this girl complaining that it's time to eat? She must never be hungry.

"Si, Alessandra! We all eat at one time together, and then we clean everything up at once. If you don't eat now, then you'll have to wait until breakfast tomorrow." The nurse drops her tray on the table next to her.

"It's only fair. We're not maids. We can't cater to everyone's appetite." The nurses chatter back and forth to each other just loud enough so we can hear them.

"I'm ready to eat," I say, hoping to turn the attention off Alessandra and onto to my grumbling stomach.

"Bene, Claudia." One nurse hands me a metal tray with a glorious helping of food; bread and pasta with beans, a small piece of meat, and an orange for dessert. It is such an indulgent meal!

I pay little attention to anything else at this point. I just want to dive into that tray with my whole body, so I forget about the pain. As soon as I try to pick up a fork, the reality of my arm in this big, clunky, heavy cast hits me. This slows me down something awful. Nevertheless, I use my left hand and enjoy my meal.

A few minutes in, I hear a very sweet voice from the other side of my bed. "The food isn't great but it's better than nothing I guess." The voice says.

Not great? I can't imagine anything better. I turn toward her, and she says, "I'm Sylvia."

She has light brown hair that is long like mine. "I hurt my foot in a bicycle accident. What happened to you?"

"I slipped on ice when I was carrying the water barrel and the metal broke my finger," I say as I wince a little, remembering the accident.

"Carrying a water barrel?" Sylvia is surprised by this.

"Yes, we need water in our house, and it's my job to get it." I turn back to my tray of food.

"Oh, I see," Sylvia doesn't push further. "Well, it's nice to meet you, *piacere!*" She turns back to her food but doesn't eat very much.

I inhale my plate of food with such enthusiasm, as if I need to finish it fast before someone takes it away. Everything tastes so delicious, different from what I usually have.

After a little while, the nurses come back around and gather up the trays. My tray is completely empty, but Alessandra's and Sylvia's are not. They ate only a little. Now the nurses are going to throw away the leftover food.

"So how long have you been here Sylvia?" I ask, wondering how long I'm going to be here.

"A month. I should be going home soon, though." Sylvia says very casually, as if it didn't faze her at all that she'd been here that long.

"A month! What about school?" I start to panic a little bit. I have to get back to school. I can't take a month off to sit in this hospital and do nothing.

"School can wait. It's not really important to me, anyway. I kind of like the break," Sylvia says.

"Well, I don't want to miss any of my schoolwork. I'm supposed to graduate soon. How am I going to keep up?" My mind is racing with thoughts. I can ask my father to bring my books, and then he could run my assignments back to the teacher. But I share my books with my sister. And the gas would be too much.

"It'll be okay, Claudia. It's not that important," Sylvia says without a care in the world. What is she planning to do with her life? I start to wonder what dreams she has. Suddenly I feel like I just want to sleep.

"Well, I think it's very important, and I'm going to figure out something. I can't fall behind because I want to go to college. They'll never take me if I don't finish high school. Sylvia, I'm feeling tired now so I'm going to sleep a little."

"Okay," says Sylvia.

I scooch down on the bed, turn to my left side and put my head on the pillow. I close my eyes and tears run down my face.

———

It's as if sunshine radiates from Dr. Blue Eyes as he enters my hospital room in the morning.

It shines light on an otherwise dark day.

I admire him and his intelligence; he helps people get better. I think about the education he must have to do this job, and it makes me miss school even more.

My hand hurts. I am upset that I'm in this hospital, alone, without anyone I know. Worst of all, I may be here for a while. I think I'm just a little cranky.

"Buon giorno, Claudia. How are you feeling today?" he says while he looks at some papers in a folder.

"I'm tired, and my hand hurts, Doctor. I didn't sleep well again last night, and I want to go home." I feel bad that I am complaining.

"Well, you can't go home just yet. We have to be able to administer the necessary medicine and monitor your condition. We can't do that if you're not here. Just get comfortable and enjoy your stay here. Did you like your dinner? I hear the food is pretty good." He speaks with an upbeat tone, trying to cheer me up.

"Yes, Doctor, the food was good, but I really would like to go home. Can you send a message to my father?" I'm pushing now.

"I'm sorry, Claudia, you really can't go. Listen, if you take all the medicine and you eat all of your food and get some rest, I promise I'll get you home as fast as possible." Dr. Blue Eyes smiles, and I relax and smile back.

I'm not really happy with this solution, but I can tell that he isn't budging, and he isn't going to send a message to my father.

"Okay, Doctor, thank you," I say defeated, lying back down. Maybe I will fall asleep again.

Alessandra is listening, and as soon as Dr. Blue Eyes walks away, she whispers, "Do you know what they do with the dead bodies around here?"

"What?" I ask, curiously.

"They feed them to us. They cut them up in tiny pieces and cook them with our dinner," she says with empty eyes as she turns her head away.

I turn to Sylvia to see if she heard what Alessandra just said, and we both giggle quietly. I think she's lost, and Sylvia gives me a look that says she agrees with me.

We have lots of days like this in the hospital. Alessandra says something strange, and Sylvia and I just laugh it off. It's all we can do to pass the time while we are there.

I feel curious about my new friend and decide to ask some questions.

"Where do you live Sylvia?" I am more interested in how but thought asking where was a better place to start.

"I live in Troia, Piazzia San Secondino. Do you know it?" Sylvia says with a smile.

"No. I live in Orsara. I've never been to Troia. Is it nice?" I say, wondering about this town that is so close to where I live but might as well be hundreds of miles away.

"It's a very nice town. I don't like that our house is close to the bottom of the hill because we have to go up for everything, but otherwise it's very nice. We're near the town cemetery. We have a big house and I love my bedroom. We have a nice garden that is my mother's pride and joy and a pretty veranda to sit under in the summer. I have a little dog named Regina," she says proudly. It sounds like a nice place.

"Tell me about your house," Sylvia says, and suddenly I feel embarrassed.

"Well, my house is big, too. We live at the top of town, so everyone has to walk up to see us. We have a big garden and lots of animals. I have a bicycle that I use to run down to the stores and pick up groceries for my mother. It has a cute little basket on the front. It's just my sister Paola and me, and she's my best friend. We are very lucky," I say, convincing myself more than Sylvia.

Although I'm not lying about Paola being my best friend. That part is true.

"Well, it sounds very nice, and maybe when we're both back home we can visit each other? Would you be allowed to come to my house?" Sylvia asks.

"Sure, I'd be allowed. My father could bring me over on our Lambretta!" I say, excited at the prospect of seeing where she lives.

We spend the rest of the afternoon talking about our towns and who our friends are. She tells me beautiful stories about her home and her little dog, and I tell her fake stories about my great life in our big house. I love hearing about Sylvia's town. It sounds so amazing and much more interesting than mine. They have festivals and celebrations and the whole town comes out.

Her town sounds much better than mine.

Before we know it, dinner is being served and tonight it is pasta with broccoli greens and some tomato salad and bread. No meat, but that's okay because I love the tomato salad. I eat all my pasta and the tomato salad, saving the best for last, dipping my bread in the leftover tomato and olive oil juice. It is so delicious that I lose myself in the fabulous taste. I moan with enjoyment, and Sylvia starts to laugh.

"What's so funny?" I ask, kind of defensively.

"Well, you seem to be enjoying that salad so much, like you've never had it before," she says, still giggling.

"I've had it before, but this salad reminds me of the one my grandmother makes for us all the time. It makes me happy since it feels like home," I say quickly.

"My mother makes a great tomato salad, too! I'll have her make it when you come over since you like it so much," Sylvia says.

We laugh some more about the tomato salad and how I was moaning. I guess it is kind of embarrassing to enjoy food so much, but she doesn't know my truth like I do.

"I'd love that!" I say as I continue to sop up every last drop with the remaining piece of bread. It has been a great day and a great dinner, but soon the nurses come around to take our trays and we get ready for bed.

I put my head down on the pillow and think about the double-edged sword that is my hospital stay. Of course, I'd rather be home with my family, but overall I have a comfortable bed to myself and meals every day.

But, I really do miss my home, despite how poor it is.

CHAPTER 8

The next morning the doctors start coming in to see each of us. We all sit up straight when they arrive; they deserve respect and we are sure to give it. I'm excited to see Dr. Blue Eyes, hoping each time it will be the day he tells me I can go home.

But, my doctor visit is disappointing. They still need to administer medicine and watch me.

Sylvia, on the other hand, gets to go home. They think her foot has healed enough, and they're not worried about her getting an infection or anything. They say they've already sent word to her parents who'll come and get her as soon as possible. How lucky she is to finally be going home!

"That's great news, Sylvia!" I say, happy for her.

I'm sure she's excited to go home and see her family, but I think in some weird way she likes it here. I know I can't wait to go home, so my excitement spills out all over the place for her. I know that hopefully I can get out soon, too!

"Yes, great news. I guess it's good that my foot is better," she says emotionless.

"Well, give me your address, and I'll write you when I get home. Then maybe we can make a plan for me to come and visit,"

I say genuinely. I really want to see her home since it sounds so beautiful. I'm hoping she never wants to come see mine.

"Okay, give me your address, too, and we'll write each other." She gets a pencil and paper from the little table next to her bed.

"Well, just give me yours first, and I'll write you with mine as soon as I get out of here. If you write me a letter now, there's no telling when I'll get it. It should be soon, right? I mean, they can't keep me here much longer, can they?" I say, changing the subject.

"Yeah, that makes sense. As soon as you get out, you'd better write. Okay?" Sylvia says hopefully.

"Of course, I will, Sylvia. I'm going to come visit as soon as I can." I secretly wonder how the heck I will get there, but I'll worry about that later.

She writes her address down and hands it to me.

"I'll write as soon as I get home and we can plan to meet again," I say as she smiles big.

"I'd love that, Claudia," Sylvia says as she starts packing her things up in a small suitcase.

Soon her mother and father arrive to get her. The nurses come in to help her gather her things and get dressed to go home while her parents wait in a room nearby. They don't let parents in here with all the patients.

She has a pretty dark-blue dress, and she wears white socks with black shoes. She looks so different in regular clothes.

"I'm going to miss you," I say as she gives me a big hug. She's lucky she's going home. I don't know how much more time I have here. And now with Sylvia leaving, it will definitely be dreary. I'll have to deal with Alessandra all on my own.

She gathers her things, and the nurses walk her out. She gets halfway down the room and turns to look back at me. She waves and her face shows me that she is happy to go but she feels bad that I have to stay.

It's okay, though. I know I'm going home soon, too.

Once Sylvia is out of sight, I settle back in my bed and turn to see Alessandra looking right at me. "I'm glad she's gone." Her dark eyes are strange looking.

"Why?" I say, ready to defend Sylvia.

"She acted like such a little princess all the time. She thinks she's better than me, and she thinks she's better than you too, Claudia."

"That's not true at all! You don't even know her. Just stop talking to me." I look in the opposite direction. She's still talking, but I ignore her. I have no interest in what she has to say.

I lie back and decide to close my eyes and think of something positive to help pass the time until we eat. I start to daydream about my home. It's small, and we don't have much, but I suddenly feel like I really need to be there. I guess I just miss my family, especially Paola. Even though we fight.

I think about a fight we had not that long ago.

I have one nice thing that I cherish—it's a monogrammed *fazzoletto*. This little handkerchief is the most special thing I own. It's a thin white cotton handkerchief, and my grandmother crocheted a pretty pink boarder around it. She sewed my initials on it so everyone in the house would know it was mine.

Paola went into my drawer and took it out one day because she wanted to carry one in her pocket. She was going to meet some friends and she lost hers, so she took mine. She lost mine when she was out in the fields hanging around with her friends, and she had no idea where it was. She felt bad, but I still got angry, and we got into a huge fight because of it.

I don't know why I'm thinking about this fight now, but it makes me restless. I miss my home and want to go back, even if my brothers and sisters are there to annoy me. I realize after spending all this time in the hospital with strangers, away from everyone I know, that I miss them and need to be home.

I'm feeling a little groggy when the nurses start coming through with dinner. I open my eyes as I smell the fresh bread and pasta with tomatoes that the nurses are carting around. As they get closer to my bed, I sit up in anticipation of what's to come.

"Claudia, we have your favorite tonight." The nurse seems excited to bring me dinner. I don't always finish my tray of food anymore, but I always look forward to what's coming. She leaves it next to my bed.

"What's for dinner?" Alessandra asks me, and I wince at the sound of her voice.

"Bread and pasta with tomatoes. Can't you see what's on your plate?" I say snapping back at her.

"Oh yes, I see! I'm starving!" Alessandra says as she starts shoveling food into her mouth.

"Alessandra, why do you eat that way? You should take your time, or your stomach will hurt." I'm mothering her now, like I do with my sisters and brothers.

"What do you mean? I'm just eating." Alessandra keeps pushing the food in.

"Well not just eating, you're eating like an animal. Slow down." I give her this advice partly because I don't want her stomach to hurt, but mostly because it makes me sick to see her eat like that. Instantly I see her embarrassment. She slows down a bit and takes one small bite at a time. Maybe she's afraid someone is going to take her food away. Maybe she has it rougher in her home than I do.

Once we finish with dinner, the nurses come around and take our trays. We only have a little bit of time left before lights out, so I read a book from the hospital library. I don't want to talk to Alessandra, anyway.

It's a book called *Nina* by Antonietta Leonardo. When the library cart came around, they told me it's about a girl who grew up in Tuscany and moved to America when she was very young. I never heard of it before, and I thought it sounded interesting so I took it.

Imagine, moving to America as a young child. Crossing the vast Atlantic Ocean to arrive in New York City! Growing up there, learning the language, going to school. My thoughts fascinate me, and I can't stop my mind from scrolling through all the possibilities.

That's an interesting idea.

I wonder how she moves to America at such a young age? And who goes with her? I get lost in the story right from the beginning.

I spend the rest of the night reading until the nurses turn off the lights. I'm so excited to pick up the book the next morning as soon as the sun starts to shine through the window. I start reading again well before the nurses come in with breakfast. The story of *Nina* is so intriguing to me.

Days pass like this where I spend my time getting medicine in my cast, eating, and reading. As I come to the end of *Nina*, I feel enlightened. I am bursting with something I can't quite describe. It is such an interesting story, and I can't believe how this family could leave everything they knew here in Italy to move to America.

It is like a dream, one that I want to pursue. I want to show this book to Paola.

Show her that it's possible to leave Italy and go to America. Show her that it can happen.

I have to bring this book home to her.

As I daydream about *Nina's* story, I am given a wonderful gift. Dr. Blue Eyes comes in and tells me it is time to remove my cast and I can go home. They feel I am ready, and I know they are right.

They called the post office in Orsara to let my parents know that I am ready to go home!

I can't wait to get out of here and go back to my family.

I can't wait to share this book with Paola.

"Alessandra, I'm going home!" I say to her as she returns from the bathroom.

"Oh, how lucky you are." She was disinterested, probably since I haven't spoken to her much at all in the last several days. But I don't care. I'm excited to get out of here and back to school.

———

A few hours later, the doctor removes my cast just before my father arrives. I say my goodbyes to Alessandra, and I try to hug her before I leave. She doesn't want to hug me. I see in her eyes that she's lost again.

"Bye, Alessandra. I hope you are well enough to go home soon, too," I say sincerely.

All I wanted to do was see my father. I gather up my few things and slip the copy of *Nina* in my shawl, hoping no one will notice. The nervousness is almost paralyzing, but I can't leave it. I hope and pray I can get out the door with it.

I walk into the waiting area, and there he is, ready to bring me home.

"Papa!" I run to him and give him a bigger hug than I ever have.

"Claudia! You look so grown up!" He picks me up off the ground and I feel my feet lift off just a little. He puts me back down fast. "You've gained some weight too; you look good and healthy! How's your finger?"

"It's fine, Papa, but it's still sensitive and they say it will probably be that way for a while. It's crooked, too, see?" I hold up my hand so he can see how my finger twists to the side.

"It's fine, Claudia, you'll be fine. Come on, let's go, everyone is home waiting for you." He grabs the few things I have, but I keep the stolen book under my arm, wrapped in my shawl. I don't want my father to see it.

We walk outside and get on the Lambretta. I hold on tightly with both hands even though my healing hand is still sensitive. I'm trying very hard to keep *Nina* close so I don't drop her. The anticipation is incredible!

We drive for what seems like an hour back to town, and I feel relief come over me. I miss my home and family so much, and now that we're getting close, I feel good. I feel peaceful, but still restless.

I know that leaving my family and this town is something I will do someday.

I will have to get used to being away from them.

We drive up the main road and the cobblestones underneath make the end of this ride more uncomfortable. We pull onto Via Silvio Pellico, and I can see my brothers and sisters waiting outside for me. They are cheering and happy and jumping up and down. My mother is standing outside the door of our house wearing her cooking apron and holding a kitchen rag in her hand.

"Grazie Dio!" I can see my mother's arms going up in the air with happiness. We pull up the street as the noise from the Lambretta echoes between the stone buildings. The neighbors come out of their homes, too.

They are outside, hanging over their balconies and clapping. It is a fantastic greeting!

"Claudia, welcome home!" I hear neighbors say as we drive by. My father is driving slowly now, so the neighbors can see that I am okay. Some pat my back as we go by.

We get to the top of the street, and my father stops in front of my mother and brothers and sisters. They all gather around me in a circle of happiness, and suddenly, all is well. I am so excited to see everyone, and they are very happy to see me.

I never thought about how much they might be missing me while I was gone.

I climb off the back of the scooter, and we all go inside to gather around the table.

Everyone has so many questions!

They want to hear all about my stay. Whom did I meet? What did they feed me? Were the doctors and nurses nice?

As soon as we get inside, I quickly take my book out from under my shawl and hide it under my pillow. Then I join everyone around the kitchen table for dinner.

We spend the rest of the evening talking all about my month-long stay in the hospital.

I tell them about Dr. Blue Eyes and the horrible pain I had.

I tell them about how great Sylvia was and how I plan on visiting her in Troia.

I tell them about Alessandra and how she seemed nice at first but then I realized she was a little lost.

But I never mention the story of Nina.

I'm saving that for Paola.

It'll be our secret.

CHAPTER 9

"Paola, look at what I brought home from the hospital," I whisper as I pull the book out from under my pillow to show her a dark brown cover with a picture of a pretty woman in a blue dress. She has a bundle on her head and a small girl by her side.

I am so tired after the scooter ride back and the long night full of questions.

But even so, I'm anxious to tell Paola about my book.

"What's this Claudia? Who gave it to you?" Paola asks. Her voice is irritated.

"Well, no one actually gave it to me, but it's a book I was reading in the hospital. It's about this girl who moves from Tuscany to America. I thought we could do the same thing?" I look at my sister carefully, waiting for her reaction.

Paola giggles quietly so not to wake anyone. "You're crazy! We can't move to America. Where would we go? How would we get the money? Mama would never let us leave!" Paola is bombarding me with excuses.

"I don't know, Paola, I've just been thinking about it. A lot." I feel a little squashed in my excitement, but that feeling is only temporary. I sit up straight and pull back my shoulders.

"You know, we can do it. And if you're too scared, than I'll do it myself." The frustration in me is building, and I don't care that she doesn't agree with my brilliant idea.

"I'm not scared, I just don't want to go that far. I don't want to stay in Orsara for the rest of my life, and we have so many great places we can go right here in Italy. What about Naples or Rome? Or even Torino if you want to go really far. It's stupid. You have no money! I mean, who's going to help you?" she says rationally.

"Well, I haven't figured out all the details yet, but one thing I know for sure, I need to finish school here so I can go to Foggia for secondary school. That's my first step." I say it definitively, as if nothing she says is going to change my mind.

"State zitti!" My mother shushes us. I put my head down on my pillow and blow out my candle.

The next morning, I get up and out of bed, feeling excited to start the day. I want to get to school. I want to finish my studies and I want to move to Foggia!

My brother Dominic is getting the water now, so my morning is a little easier. I get dressed in my school uniform, help my sisters get ready and out the door I go without Paola. She's moving too slowly, and I don't want to be late on my first day back.

It's such a beautiful morning! It's chilly out, but the sun is shining, and I can feel its warmth in my body. I suddenly feel excited about the possibility of getting away from here. Wouldn't it be great to live in America?

The land where anything can happen,
where everyone has food and money,
where everyone has a job.

I can see myself now, in a beautiful coat and pretty shoes.

Walking down the street in New York City and seeing all the big buildings I only know about from the newspapers.

I imagine there's so much to be happy about in America, and I can't wait to get there.

I skip my way down the cobblestones very much in my own head. I can't stop thinking beautiful thoughts of America that I barely see Mrs. Grasso as I walk by her.

"Buon giorno, Claudia?" she says as if she's asking me if it's good morning.

I want to say, Yes!

Yes! It's a good morning!

But instead I keep it simple.

"Si, Signora Grasso! It's a good day, and I'm going to school," I say as I hear her grumble under her breath that school is a waste of time for girls.

Walking through town, I feel light on my feet. I'm happy as I pass the Fontana and even happier to be done with the chore of getting water.

As I walk into the school courtyard, I notice that a lot of kids are already there. The girls are standing around together, snickering and looking at the group of boys on the other side. The boys are kicking stones and being boisterous, trying to get the girl's attention.

I walk over to the girls and hear them talking about our teacher.

"Well, I heard she's going to have a baby!" Rosa says to the group, extremely proud of herself for knowing this top-secret information. Rosa always has gossip about everyone, so I guess it's not surprising that she's the one speaking up about our teacher.

"No way! She's not even married, and she couldn't possibly be pregnant. Where did you hear that, Rosa?" I'm irritated and getting angry.

"Hi, Claudia!" Rosa says to change the subject. "How are you? How was the hospital? Are you all better now?" she asks as she looks at my hand. I have it wrapped to protect it, but also to hide it.

"I'm fine, Rosa. The hospital was fine, too. Now what are you gossiping about?" I say, still irritated.

"I heard from my mother who heard it from someone in town who knows her boyfriend. Apparently, she's trying to keep it a secret, but it's getting out. She'll probably be forced to leave school soon. You watch!" Rosa says with confidence.

"Oh, shut up Rosa. You're so wrong! There's no way that's true." I say as we all start walking into the school building. Everyone lines up quickly and quietly and in we go.

There's no way Rosa knows what she's talking about.

I like Maestra Corrado. She's always nice to me, and she helps me out a lot. Probably because she knows we are poor, and I love school. I think for a minute that I might tell her about my book, but I can't explain where it came from, so I change my mind. I always love coming to school. Mostly because I love my teacher, but also because the opportunities are endless. I have so much to learn, and the more I learn the further I can go.

The schoolroom is filling up with kids, and everyone begins to take a seat on benches facing the chalkboard. The room is buzzing with the usual morning excitement; everyone is happy to see each other. The teacher claps her hands loudly to get us under control.

"Come children, it's time to work. Claudia, welcome back! Now everyone take out your religion book, Don Tommaso is coming for our lesson today," Maestra Corrado says as our priest enters the room.

"Buon giorno! Buon giorno!" Don Tommaso says to the class. He's a nice priest, not much older than Paola, and all the kids like him. He walks around town on Sundays playing a flute to remind us all that it's time for mass. The kids come out of their homes and follow him to church.

I like when he comes to teach us. When he talks about the bible, it's poetic. His stories are interesting, and I hang on every word he says as he walks around the front of the class, talking about Jesus and God in a very theatrical way.

After religion, Maestra Corrado teaches us mathematics and history until lunch.

We all grab our lunch baskets and start to walk outside. We get a little time to go to the bathroom, eat our meal, and entertain each other before we have to come back inside for the afternoon session. Before I leave the class, Maestra Corrado calls me to her desk.

"Claudia, I'd like to speak with you." I pick up my things and walk toward her. For a moment I think she might have heard the school yard gossip and is going to ask me about it. My face gets red.

"Claudia, how are you feeling? I was so sad about your accident and that you had to miss so much school. Is your hand okay now?" She seems very concerned.

"I'm okay. My hand is still so sensitive but it's getting better. I'm just happy to be back at school. I need to do a lot of work to catch up," I say, making sure she knows that I'm determined.

"Well, you are very smart. I see you answering questions easily that make most kids stumble. I'm sure you'll be able to catch up and maybe think about what you want to do after primary school is over." She gives me hope and makes me feel comfortable in sharing my secret dreams with her.

"Well, I want to go to school in Foggia, maybe go to college and become a teacher or a doctor. And then I want to move to America. I want to go to New York City!" I say excitedly, spilling it all out to her.

Her mouth falls open a little as if she isn't sure what to think or say. She hesitates for a minute and then says, "Well that is a superb goal, Claudia. I think having big dreams is a great thing. And I believe you are just a hard enough worker to do it. But it won't be easy, you know, getting to America that is. That's a really big goal and you'll have a lot of obstacles standing in your way." She says it gently. She knows it's a crazy dream, just like my mother and sister do, but in my eyes, she can tell I'm serious.

"I know it won't be easy, but I have to try. I can't see myself living in this town for the rest of my life. There's so much to see and do in the world! I just feel like I have to get out there." I try to convince her of how important it is to me.

"Well, that's what I wanted to talk with you about. See, with your intelligence and desire for more, I think you should really consider being a midwife in town. Or you can study to be a nurse, maybe in the Female Assistance Corp in the military. They give you uniforms, food, and a place to stay. Then you can travel all around and see different places, meet all kinds of people while helping others," Maestra says.

"I know of scholarships for school that I can help you apply for. What do you think about that?" My teacher looks intently at me, and I know she is anxious to see my reaction to her suggestion.

I think about it a little bit before I answer. I don't want to be a midwife in town or a nurse. I want to be a doctor. I do like the idea of traveling around and seeing different places, and the military would give me that opportunity. But do I really want to be in the military? Only the boys are required to do that, and it doesn't sound like something I would enjoy.

"Hmm, Maestra Corrado, I think this is all something I really need to think about. But I thought only the boys went into the military?" I say curiously.

"Well, of course, military time is mandatory for the boys, but this branch is for female volunteers and that might be interesting for you. They have positions, like nursing, that girls can do. It's just a thought, don't worry too much about it now. You have a lot of catching up to do before you can graduate. Go out and get a little free time to eat your lunch before our next session. We can talk more about this another time." Maestra Corrado stands to leave.

"Okay," I say as I grab my basket from her desk. "Thank you. And thanks for saying that I'm smart." I smile and walk toward the door. I didn't think this day could get any better, but when your teacher tells you that you're smart, that's pretty much like the Pope saying it. It must be true.

We have very little time left before we have to come in for the afternoon session. I hurriedly eat my lunch and have a few giggles with my friends before we head back inside. I'm feeling very hopeful. I really can't wait to finish my schooling here so I can go to Foggia.

One step closer to my American Dream!

CHAPTER 10

———

The school is chilly today, but the light from the sun shines through the windows to warm up the room. It's early and I'm here alone enjoying the quiet stillness. I fell so far behind because of the accident that I need to do a lot of work to graduate on time. The reading is easy for me, but I have to spend extra time with Maestra Corrado, especially in mathematics. I can't teach that to myself.

But today is a special day! Zia Lucia is coming from America to visit us!

I know her only by the one photograph my father has of her from when they were young and the neat brown packages tied with white string we receive a few times a year. But today, I will finally get to meet her. She's coming, and I'm jumping out of my skin.

It's getting close to the start of school, and too cold to stay outside. The other kids start coming inside, and Paola comes in and sits next to me.

"Paola, aren't you excited for today?" I ask. She looks at me confused, not sure what to be excited about.

"You know! Zia Lucia is coming to visit us from America!" I say obviously.

"Oh that. I guess it's exciting. I hope she brings us something." Paola looks away as if she couldn't care less.

"Aren't you interested in seeing her in person? We've only seen her picture and you can't tell anything from a picture. She can tell us so much about America!" I was almost breathless with my excitement.

"Why do you care so much, Claudia? She's just coming for a short visit, and it's not that exciting." Paola is so disinterested. She doesn't even pretend to care a little about having a relative from America come to our house.

"Well, I'm very excited. And I care because I want to go to America someday and—"

Paola cuts me off. "I know, I know." She rolls her eyes. "You think you're going to leave Orsara and go to school and move to America. I get it." Her voice is dull.

I think about her sarcasm and also what my teacher said. How can I accomplish this big dream? Maybe I am being naive to think I can do this? I don't have a plan, just some big idea that I'm not sure how to implement.

"It's my dream and I can dream whatever I want. It's fine if you plan on spending your life in this town, but that's not what I want," I say strongly. I can talk to Zia Lucia about it when she gets here. I'm sure she won't think it's a stupid idea.

———

I impatiently go through the usual routines at school, huffing and puffing to get out the door and up the street toward home as quickly as possible. My steps are light but determined. I am hopping over the cracks in the stones like I'm playing hopscotch. I am elated and can't wait to get home.

As soon as I turn up my street, I see some people standing around outside our house.

It's a big deal to get visitors at all let alone from America, and there she is, standing like a famous movie star.

She has on a beautiful hat, long overcoat, and black-heeled shoes that must have been very difficult to walk in on the cobblestones. I've never seen shoes like that in person. I walk up the street, and my mother sees me. I can tell that she's excited to introduce me to Zia Lucia, so I start running up to her, arriving breathless.

"Ciao Zia! I'm Claudia!" I have a smile from ear to ear as I give her a big hug. She smells like perfume, and her coat is soft. She feels like she's the same size as my mother, a little round in the middle.

"Ciao Claudia. I've heard so much about you from your mother. She's very proud of you, you know. She says you do very well in school." Zia Lucia shocks me with this information. I never knew my mother was proud of me.

I blush a little, embarrassed by the attention as I say, "Thank you."

Zia Lucia turns to my mother and says, "Josefina, your daughter is so beautiful. Look at this gorgeous hair! Such a beautiful dark brown and so full." She compliments me further.

I instantly fall in love with this woman from America. She appears to be everything I want to be and she's here in front of me.

My mother interrupts my thoughts, "Come on, everyone, let's go inside!" She wants to get out of the neighbors' view. The drawback of living in such close quarters.

Zia Lucia goes to pick up her bags, but very quickly my brothers take them from her to bring them inside. I see her take a very slow, long look around before we walk inside, and I realize that no one has ever come to visit us before. Embarrassment creeps into me.

"Josefina, your children have such beautiful manners," Zia Lucia says to my mother. Then she turns to the boys and says, "Thank you so much for your help." The boys smile widely and struggle to carry her bags, which look to be larger than they are, inside.

Inside the kids are all scurrying around, and my mother is yelling at the boys to bring Zia's bags to the back of the house. My father pulls up a chair for her at the table and asks for her coat. I don't know when he last saw his half sister, but they quickly get comfortable with each other.

We had been preparing for her visit all month, so we had plenty of firewood to keep the house warm and fresh water and flour to make pasta. My parents wanted everything to be perfect for her visit.

Zia Lucia hands my father her coat and falls into the chair as if she walked here from America. Looking at those shoes, I'm sure her feet are hurting something awful. She looks around a little more and then her gaze fixes on mine. She's trying to hide her feelings about what she sees, but she knows I can see it.

"Josefina, this is a nice home you've made. It's very warm and cozy," she says with an air about her. She is fancy; I can see that. She wears nice clothes and shoes and smells good. Her hair is perfectly done, and she even has some makeup on. If this is how America treats you, I definitely want to go there.

"Grazie, Lucia," my mother says, feeling happy but aware that Lucia is probably just saying that to be nice.

Paola walks in after taking her sweet time coming home from school.

"This is Paola, my oldest daughter. And our firstborn. She helps me a lot with the younger children and all the chores," my mother says. I can tell she's proud of Paola, too.

"Very nice to meet you, Paola. It sounds like you are a big help around here. What's your favorite job to do?" Zia Lucia asks, making conversation.

"Well, none of them really. I don't like doing chores, and someday I won't have to do them anymore," she says confidently.

"Really, how will you manage that?" Zia Lucia asks quizzically.

"Well, I'm going to marry a man who will take care of me, of course. Then we can hire someone to do the chores for us," Paola says snobbishly.

"And what will you do, Paola?" Zia Lucia seemed to be forming an opinion about my sister.

It wasn't a good one.

"I'll take care of the children. And maybe the garden and the animals if we live on a farm. I know how to do those things, too." Paola quickly changes direction and says, "I love your shoes! How do you walk in them?"

Zia Lucia breaks out in a laugh and says, "Well it's not easy on these streets!" We all break out in laughter.

She kicks them off and motions for Paola to put them on. Paola jumps at the chance. She slips on those beautiful black-heeled shoes and starts walking around our home. She's strutting with an air of confidence that I've never seen.

Now she looks like a movie star!

I need to get a pair of those shoes.

"Claudia, tell me about school. I hear you like it a lot," Zia Lucia says as she crosses her legs and rubs one foot.

"Oh, I absolutely love school. I mean not necessarily my school, but I love learning and all my subjects. My favorite is probably math, but I love learning about art and language and even religion. Don Tommaso is our priest. He comes to teach us religion, and he makes it fun." I'm rattling on and on.

"It's so exciting and interesting to learn new things. I want to graduate from my school here in Orsara and then go to Foggia for secondary school. I'm not sure what I want to do yet, but my teacher suggested nursing in the Female Assistance Corp." I want to keep going but I stop since it looks like Zia Lucia has something to say.

"That is an interesting path to take, but maybe we should explore a few others. You can be a teacher. You seem very smart and love to learn, and that makes for a great teacher." Zia Lucia smiles at me with hope.

"I don't know, yet, but I know I can't wait to go to school in Foggia. My teacher says she can help me apply for a scholarship to pay for it, so I'm working really hard to keep my grades up." I'm proud to tell Zia Lucia this.

"That's a good idea. And I'm sure you'll be able to go to school the way you want to. But you know right now I would love to get cleaned up after my long trip." Zia Lucia looks at my mother wondering exactly how that can happen.

"Claudia and Paola will get a small bath ready for you so you can freshen up. Come on, girls, go get some water to warm on the fire." She says it with a calm, sweet tone that I'm not used to hearing.

My sister and I jump up and do what our mother says. She's usually very tough, but she was being a little nicer to us in front of Zia Lucia. I like having her here.

We grab our galvanized tub that we use for washing up and doing laundry in the winter. We bring it to the back of the house where the beds are and begin to heat some water on the fire. We mix a comfortable combination of cold and boiling hot water to make a nice bath for Zia Lucia. We grab a couple of rags and a sheet to wrap around her. My sister and I take pride in helping her wash up. We used the rags to clean her face, arms, and feet. We wanted her to feel like a queen in our house.

"You girls are so good to me. You really make me feel special in your home. Thank you for taking care of me. I really am tired from my trip, and this just makes me feel wonderful," Zia Lucia says, happy and relaxed.

"You're welcome," we say. We don't have much to offer her except respect and a pleasant stay.

I'm so grateful that she's here, and I want to ask her about America but I'm not sure it's the right time. I want to find a way to talk about my dream of living there someday.

"Do you girls ever think about coming to America some-day? You could come and visit me when you're a little older, you know?" My heart is jumping out of my body that she actu-ally just brought it up. But before I can answer, Paola chimes in.

"Claudia thinks she's going to move there." She rolls her eyes as she finishes that sentence. "I mean, I think it would be nice to visit, but I like living here. And I couldn't leave everyone behind like that." Paola says in a superior tone.

"I never said I wanted to leave everyone behind!" I say defensively. "I just want to get out of this town, and I think moving to America is the dream of a lifetime! And maybe we can all go, our whole family, you know?" I say this, not knowing what my family thinks about that idea. Other than Paola. But I didn't want to look like a girl who could abandon her whole family.

"I think it's a great idea. In fact, after coming here to visit, I would really like to help you do that. I'll talk to your mother about it, and maybe we can figure out a plan together." Zia Lucia winks at me.

"Oh, Zia, that would be the best thing ever!" I say excitedly and as I look at Paola. She rolls her eyes again. I imagine she thinks it's a pipe dream and we'll never hear anything about it again, but I am determined to be involved in the conversation my mother and my aunt are going to have about it.

We finish helping her clean up and then we leave her alone to get dressed. We go to help our mother finish dinner preparations, and I mention our conversation to her.

"Mama, Zia Lucia says maybe we could go visit her in America." I am cautious in my wording.

"Claudia, don't be crazy. We don't have the money to travel to America, even for a short visit. There's too many of us, and it would be too expensive." But I see her thinking about it as if she would love to take that trip.

"But Mama, we have to figure something out. Maybe I can get a job and start saving some money for the trip. Paola can, too." I offer my mother a solution.

"I don't want to get a job so we can go to America. We'd have to work years to save enough money for that." Paola is annoyed that I would even bring her into this.

"Shhh, girls, come on, don't embarrass us." My mother whispers so Zia Lucia doesn't hear. "She has good intentions, but I don't think it would work," my mother says dismissively.

Just then Zia Lucia joins the conversation, "Oh come on, Josefina, I'm sure we can figure something out. We just need a plan, and maybe you can come over a few at a time. Life would be so much better." My aunt stresses that point.

"But we don't speak English. How would we get jobs? How will we support ourselves?" my mother asks realistically as I hang on every word.

"English can be learned. Besides, there are plenty of places in America where lots of Italians work. Like factories. There are a bunch in the bigger cities that employ immigrants. We'd just have to find one that has mostly Italians so you could work with people like yourselves. Then you can make money and gradually learn English. That's how it's done." Zia Lucia makes it sound so easy.

"Well, we still don't have any money to get us there. Come on, Lucia, let's not fill these girl's heads with crazy dreams. We're about to have dinner; girls go round up your brothers and sisters." My mother was in charge and of course we listen and do what she says. I don't want to leave this conversation, but I see in my mother's eyes that it is time for us to go.

As soon as my mother thinks we can't hear her, she starts to mumble something to my aunt that sounds a little annoyed and angry. Zia Lucia is defending herself, but that's all I can make out. I keep walking out the front door.

Oh America! Moving there is such a dream, and maybe I'm crazy and maybe I can't do it but now I feel like I must try!

Paola is ahead of me, and I run a little to catch up to her.

―――――――

We round up the kids and get them back to the house. It's time for dinner, and everyone has to be there and on their best behavior in front of Zia Lucia. Mama prepares the best meal she can, pasta with white beans and greens. She made some fresh bread and made sure to have some fruit and nuts for dessert.

We never have dessert, but Mama wanted to make a good impression on Zia Lucia.

My father takes the younger kids out for a walk so the women can spend some time catching up. Paola and I sit in the back to give them some privacy, but we still can hear everything. Our mother and Zia Lucia laugh together and drink some wine. They talk about the families, and Mama asks our aunt about her life in America. Zia Lucia tells her she's content. She has a nice house, and her husband is a good man. This makes my mother happy.

It's interesting to see my mother like this. Like a regular woman having a good time chatting with another woman, instead of a tired mother working so hard to take care of her large family. I've never seen her this way; usually, she has no time to spend with friends.

My father returns, and everyone is tired from our big day. We crowd together in a small sleeping space so Zia Lucia can have more room to sleep. We all go to bed content and happy.

The next morning, I hear Zia Lucia wake early and so I follow her to the kitchen table. I want some time with her myself.

"Buon giorno, Zia," I say sleepily.

"Buon giorno, Claudia. How did you sleep?" Zia Lucia asks.

"I slept fine, but how did you sleep? I'm sorry if it wasn't as comfortable as what you're used to."

"Oh, don't apologize, it was perfectly fine. I slept very well. I think I was just so tired from the excitement of the whole day. Actually, the whole trip has been exhausting," she says as she takes a deep breath. "I had a lot of people to visit in my short time here, and your family is my last stop. I head home after this."

"I know, Zia, and I'm so happy you came here to see us. I admire you so much, and I really want to see America someday." I think I can trust her, so I share my book with her.

"You know, Zia, I have this book called *Nina*. I got it from the hospital when I hurt my hand. It's about a young girl who moves to America with her family, and it's where I first got the idea." I go back to get my book so I can show it to her.

She looks it over and says, "Well I haven't read it, but I must pick up a copy. I'd love to read any book you recommend!" She says in a way that fills me up with pride. I suddenly have a great idea.

"Oh Zia, I would love to lend you my book to take back to America with you. You know, as a souvenir."

"Oh, Claudia this is too special. I couldn't take it."

"Yes, please, you'll make me so happy if you take it. I've already read it, and nothing would make me happier than to know you have my book in America. And, you can give it back to me when I come and visit you someday." I say confidently.

Please take it!" I push the book to her, and she can see in my eyes that I'm not taking no for an answer.

"Okay, Claudia, I will happily take your book and read it from cover to cover." She says smiling.

"Thank you, Zia. You couldn't have made me happier. Now I have to get ready for school," I say, jumping up with more energy than usual.

———

We have a couple of beautiful days with Zia Lucia, but her visit is coming to an end, and she begins preparations to go back home. I feel very sad as her departure is approaching, but I know she has to go. I hope I see her again someday. I hope I see her in America.

We help her get to the center of town with her bags. A taxi is coming to get her, and that's the closest he can get to our house. It's on our way to school, anyway, and I want to spend every last minute with her.

"Zia, I hate that you're leaving." I feel on the verge of tears as I give her one last big hug. It's the start of the day and the street is full of people. I don't want to cry.

"It's okay, Claudia. You will come and see me in America. I know it!" And with that vote of confidence, I feel the rock in my stomach starting to dissolve.

I take a deep breath and instantly feel better.

She's right, I have nothing to be sad about.

I say my goodbyes, tell her I'll see her soon, and take off for school.

It's a beautiful day, and I feel funny, like everything is different inside me now.

Now I have a goal.

A real goal.

It's going to be hard, but I'm going to do it anyway.

CHAPTER 11

————

I get to school and immediately go to my desk.

Class has already begun, and everyone has their books open.

"Claudia, you're late!" Maestra Corrado says with an annoyed tone of voice.

"Yes, I'm sorry, my aunt was leaving to go back to America. I wanted to help her with her bags," I say, hoping she asks me about my American relative since all I want to do is talk about her. But she doesn't.

"Fine, well, let's begin then." She starts on the lesson for the day. I'm not very interested in what she's talking about, but it's almost the end of the school year, and I'm going to graduate. My mind starts to wander away from this classroom, away from whatever my teacher is saying. I think about what the future holds, and I feel excited.

I think about Paola. She's not graduating with me but she doesn't seem to care. I wish she would come with me to Foggia, but that's not an option for her.

School goes on as usual, and the next few weeks seem to drag along. I make sure to finish all my work quickly and correctly. I even finished all the work I missed when I was in the hospital, so there's nothing holding me back from graduating.

I have a plan for my future now and I'm anxious to move on.

All the graduates are.

It's now the last week of school, and my teacher pulls me aside. "Claudia, have you thought about what you're going to do next? What are your plans?" she asks, knowing that most kids get jobs in town, or maybe in a nearby town, and plan on getting married. She knows that's not my plan.

"Yes! I'm going to Foggia. As soon as school ends here, I'm going to work a little to make enough money to travel. Then in September I'll be ready to go." I know I didn't get the scholarship because of my accident so I've already figured out another plan. I'm sure of myself, no doubt whatsoever.

"Good. And your parents are okay with this?" she asks.

"Yes, of course. I've worked out all the details with them, and they support me 100 percent," I lie. My mother knows of my dreams, but she hasn't completely agreed on a plan. I never mentioned it to my father, and I'm pretty sure my mother hasn't, either.

"Well I'm glad to hear you have a plan, but be careful. Foggia is a much bigger town, and you can get in trouble there. You can't trust everybody you meet. Be smart about who you talk to," she says thoughtfully.

I assure her that I understand. I know it's a bigger town than what I'm used to, and I know what I'm doing.

I thank her for her advice and hand in the last of my work for her to check.

She looks through it quickly and smiles.

I know it's all correct and so does she.

The day finally arrives! Mama makes sure my uniform is clean and neat.

And I put it on for one last time.

The sun is shining, the birds are chirping, and a beautiful warm breeze brushes past me on my way to school. I am comforted by the warmth of the sun, yet I get chills at the thought of what's to come.

Only five of us are graduating, so we get to school a few minutes early to talk in the courtyard. We are all excited; Paola and the younger kids are envious.

"What are you going to do now, Claudia?" Rosa asks curiously. She's graduating, too, and I know she's just being nosy.

"I'm going to work for the summer to save money so I can go to school in Foggia in September," I say.

Rosa laughs out loud as if she was just told the funniest joke. She's holding her stomach and being very dramatic about it. Paola scowls at her.

"And why are you laughing?" I ask angrily, my face twisting in disgust at her reaction.

"What are you thinking, Claudia? You can't go to school in Foggia. Where would you get the money? And I know your mother will never let you," Rosa says. As much as I hate to admit it, she's right.

"I have it all worked out. There's no way I'm staying here for any longer than I have to," I say, determined to make my point. "There's so much out there, Rosa. Aren't you curious?"

"Sure, but I don't think I could ever leave. It's scary out there. Besides, my family is here. Your family is here. Did you think about that?" she asks.

"Oh, shut your mouth, Rosa. You don't know anything about my sister or our family," Paola says in my defense.

I smile and say, "Rosa, I'm not planning on leaving my family forever. I want to get them out of this town, too. I just need to get my degree first so I can get a good job. Make enough money to move everyone out." Rosa listens carefully, rethinking her opinion.

At that moment, Maestra Corrado comes out and calls to us. "Andiamo, let's go. Come on kids, line up to come inside."

We all line up as usual, us graduates and all the younger kids, too. We walk inside in a line the way we have almost every other day, but this was the last day for me. I'm walking on clouds, knowing that I am done with primary school, and I'll be going to Foggia soon.

"Take your seats quietly, and let's get started. Today is a big day. As you know, we have five students graduating today. They are finished with primary school and now have some life choices to make. Some will stay in town and get jobs, some will get jobs in other towns, and at least one of you will go to secondary school." My teacher winks at me as she says that.

"I want you all to know that I'm very proud of all that you have accomplished and wish you well in whatever you chose to do in your life," Maestra Corrado says as she picks up a small stack of papers.

She calls each of our names, and we walk up and get our certificates. I am so proud and so happy as my teacher hands it to me. The paper is thick and creamy white. An ornate scrolled border surrounds the edges, and there's a red seal in the lower right corner. I look down and see my name.

Claudia Valentino.

Proudly written in black ink.

With a grin from ear to ear, I say thank you and walk back to my seat. After the ceremony is over, the rest of the class erupts in excitement. They are all clapping and congratulating us.

I am exploding with happiness.

School is over for the summer, and everyone is ready to go out and enjoy the sun.

This is just the beginning for me.

I'm ready for bigger and better things!

———————

Now I need money.

The very next day I walk over to the ovens where all the bread in town is baked. I know the baker because he comes around town to pick up loaves of dough and bring them to the ovens. Then when they are ready, he delivers them. It isn't the best place to work in town, but I know he always needs help.

As I get closer, the scent of baking bread is delicious, and it makes me smile. Warm and inviting, it feels good to be near it. The smells fill my stomach, and I don't feel so hungry.

I see the baker pushing a cart with wood toward the ovens.

"Ciao Signore. I'm Claudia Valentino," I say happily.

"I know you. Your family has all those kids on Via Silvio Pellico, right?" He says in disdain.

It's embarrassing. Everyone knows we have no money, and yet we have so many kids.

My mother has been pregnant every year for as long as I can remember.

I dismiss his comment and ask, "Do you need any help here? I'm looking for work." I try to look strong and able so he'll hire me.

Laughing, he says, "What can you do here? I need someone who can lift heavy things and help with picking up and delivering bread." He looks at my deformed hand and winces.

"I'm a lot stronger than I look. I can go get wood and hay for the fire. Just let me try."

"No, go home. We have no job for you here. I can't have a girl around here trying to do this job. It's too hard." He shoos me away with one hand and goes back to work. He's sweating profusely while he stacks wood on a cart to take into the ovens.

"Please sir, I'd like to try. If you don't like the way I do the job today, then don't pay me, and I won't come back."

He sighs, looks me up and down and thinks about it. He looks tired, and I'm thinking maybe he really needs help.

"Please, just today I will help you." I'm almost pleading. I just want to start working right away. I feel a sense of urgency to get a job and start making money.

He takes a deep breath. "Well. I'm working alone today so it can't hurt. Just don't hurt yourself because I'm not paying any hospital bills." He says in a nasty tone.

"Thank you so much, Signore," I say, eager to start working.

He tells me the jobs that need to be done, and I can already see where I am going to be most useful. They use wood and hay to keep the fires going, so I offer to go get the hay. I know it needs to be done and he has no one else around to do it right now.

I grab a large cotton cloth and go off into the fields. I lay the cloth down and put the hay on it in long lines. I fill this cloth up so it's three times my size, tie up the ends, and lift it up onto my back just at my shoulders. I'm holding the bottom of the bale so it doesn't slip off as I walk it back to the ovens.

The baker sees me coming and runs after me.

"I'm okay, don't touch it. It'll spill everywhere if you touch it so wait until we get back," I say quickly.

He listens and appears to be amazed at how much I'm able to carry. I'm not going to lie, my body aches from it. But if this is what it takes, then so be it.

"Claudia, you're going to hurt yourself carrying that much at once!" But he smiles in surprise and says, "Good job!"

He's already happy that I can do more than he thought, and then I make a few more trips, this time making the bales a little bit smaller so I won't hurt myself. He's still impressed.

I spend my day doing whatever jobs need to be done. The ovens throw off an unimaginable amount of heat, and it's wearing me down. The day comes to an end, and I'm grateful.

"Claudia, you surprised me today. You are a very hard worker, and I can use a girl like you around here. You don't mind doing any job that needs to be done, and I like that about you," he says, and I feel my posture straighten even more with pride.

"Thank you, sir. I need the work so I'll do any job I can," I say sincerely.

"Well, that's good because I need the help. You come back tomorrow and work again." He hands me a loaf of warm bread to bring home. I feel proud that I did such a good job, and I'm so happy that I can go back tomorrow.

"Oh, thank you! And thanks for the bread. I'll be here first thing in the morning!" I say excitedly, running off toward home.

———

I show up for my job early in the morning, and I do this several days a week. I need to get wood, too, but he says I can use the cart for that. Each week I gather wood and hay for the ovens, and he pays me.

On the days I get paid, he also gives me a small loaf of bread to bring home.

That loaf of bread makes my family happy, and I feel good bringing it to them.

Every week when I get home with my pay, I wrap the money in a handkerchief and hide it in a hole in the wall near my bed. It isn't a lot, but it's a start. I've already saved a good amount, and I've been trying to calculate how much I need for the trip. I need enough for the bus trip to Foggia. The school gives you a place to sleep, so I'll probably just need money for books and maybe food. I can get a job there and work when I'm not in class. I write it all down in my little booklet.

The weeks go by quickly, and I feel proud that I'm making my own money.

Working at the ovens is heavy work, and I feel like I'm getting stronger. But this week I'm definitely feeling worn out. I'm very happy when the baker says I can go home early. He pays me my week's wages and hands me another warm loaf of bread. It feels good in my hands as I hold it up to my face and take a long breath in. I close my eyes and savor every moment.

"Delizioso, vero?" he asks, and I answer quickly.

"Oh, yes sir, it is delicious Thank you for your kindness." I say as I walk away. I want to get home and add my wages to my handkerchief. I need to lay it all out and see how much I have now. I feel peaceful as I walk home in the summer heat.

When I get home, I quickly go to my handkerchief to add my money to the rest.

Someone has touched it!

I open the handkerchief and half of my money is missing. I start screaming.

"We've been robbed!" I yell loudly for everyone to hear.

My brothers and sisters all look up in shock.

"Oh my God, really? Who could have robbed you?" Paola says in disbelief.

"Claudia, Elena's shoes were falling apart, and your father hasn't been getting any work lately. I'll give it back to you after he gets paid," my mother says, dismissing the whole thing as if it were no big deal.

I know what that means.

I'll never get that money back.

"Mama, this is my money for school!" I say, screaming angrily and on the verge of tears. "Why would you take my money for her shoes?"

"Claudia, don't be so selfish. Your sister is walking on stones, her shoes are so bad. I told you I'd pay you back. You'll have enough money for school, anyway." She dismisses me.

"You really are being selfish, Claudia; Mama didn't take that much money," Paola says, siding with our mother.

I am furious.

I can see my mother getting mad, too, and about to lose her patience, but I don't care.

"You'll never pay that money back. You don't even want me to go to school!" I'm still screaming, and I think the whole town can hear me.

My mother comes over and grabs my arm.

She squeezes very tightly and gets in my face with her anger.

"You are not going to Foggia if you act like this. We need the money you are making to help us with the family!" she says in an angry voice, as if I have no right to protest.

"I never asked for all these brothers and sisters. Why do I have to pay for them? You're the one who wanted to have all these kids!" I'm letting it all out. I'm so tired of taking care of kids.

"Claudia, I didn't take all of your money, but I will if you keep acting this way." My mother threatens me, and I realize I have to be more careful now.

I take my handkerchief with what was left of my money and storm out of the house. I'm furious that I did that backbreaking, crappy work all this time for my sister to get a new pair of shoes.

I'm crying, I feel ill, and there's nothing I can do to get that money back.

I walk around town by myself for a little while.

I finally find a quiet place to sit and think about everything.

"Claudia, is that you?" I hear a voice coming up from behind me. I'm so lost in my thoughts that I hardly noticed him on his bike until he was right next to me.

"Marcello, what are you doing here?" I ask as I snap out of my fog.

"My mother needs something from the market for dinner, so I told her I'd ride over to get it. I don't have a lot of time since she's in the middle of cooking. How are you? Why are you sitting here alone?" he asks curiously.

"Oh, I just needed to get away from my family. I'm just having a bad day," I say, not wanting to tell him what really happened.

"Well, whatever it is, I'm sure you'll realize that it's no big deal and you can work it out," he says confidently as he starts to cycle away from me.

"Wait, Marcello!" I yell, and he stops his bike and turns back to me.

"Thank you!" I kiss my hand and blow it in his direction.

He smiles and continues away.

I think about what he said, and he's right. I decide I need a better hiding place, and I'll just work harder to make more money. I get home and go to my bed. I just want to be alone and quiet. I don't even get up to eat dinner and no one bothers me. As soon as everyone is asleep, I look around for a new place I can hide my handkerchief.

I find a hole behind the one dresser we have in our house. I put it there and pray no one finds it.

I continue to go to work every day through the rest of the summer, never missing an opportunity to make money. Every day the work is hard, but the baker pays me well, and I am happy that so far no one has found my new hiding place. I manage to save enough money despite my mother never paying me back for Elena's shoes.

I ask people in town, anyone who knows someone who went to school in Foggia, about when it starts. I get information from the bar about a bus ticket. I've been preparing all summer, and now it's September. I'm so excited for my trip.

I just want to go to school, to learn, to think, to find something bigger than myself.

It is Saturday morning and school starts on Monday. I already packed the few things I own, a pair of socks, some walnuts, extra underwear, my writing booklet, and one dress I took from Paola. I wrote a note for Paola, so she doesn't worry, and also to apologize for taking her dress.

I leave early, before anyone wakes up, mostly so they can't stop me or make me feel stupid for going.

The house is quiet and peaceful. No one moves at all, and no one seems to notice the little bit of noise I am making. I open the door as quietly and slowly as I can to avoid any creaking noises, and I think I am successful. I manage to get on the other side of it, close it, and no one is the wiser.

As I step outside, I notice that the morning is mild, and even this early, delicious smells waft from the neighbors' homes. People are already preparing for the day, and I feel a sense of hope in the air. It isn't too far to Foggia, just over an hour by bus. I walk to town to get a ticket and then down to the bottom of town to the bus stop. My feet are twisting sideways on the cobblestones I know so well, and I am nervous.

Nervous about getting caught and nervous about not getting caught.

I want to go so badly, but I'm scared to leave the only town I've ever known. Alone.

I wish Paola was coming with me.

But she hasn't graduated yet and even after she does, she already said she's done with school. All my people, my family, everyone is here, and I have spent my entire life here up until now. I'm just seventeen years old.

The town is quiet. It's pretty early, but the bar is open where I can get the bus ticket. I run into an old lady whose name I don't know. She looks me up and down, and I can see her wheels turning in her mind. She's wondering what I'm doing out so early with a small suitcase in my hand. She can tell I'm going somewhere, and she wants to ask but doesn't.

"Buon giorno, how are you?" I say just to be polite. She looks miserable, yet she seems to want to talk to me.

"Eh, I'm okay. My legs and hands hurt all the time and I can hardly sleep anymore but eh, la vecchiaia."

I know what she means: "That's old age."

We have a lot of old people in town, so I hear this phrase often. I think it's a good thing, though. It means we live a healthy lifestyle. Maybe it's the food, or the uphill walks, or the fresh air. Orsara is a small town, but it's doing something right.

I smile and keep walking past her so I won't have to get into any further conversation. I go into the bar to buy the bus ticket.

I open my handkerchief and use a good portion of my savings for the ticket. I don't buy anything else.

It's getting light out, and the bus will be at the stop in thirty minutes.

I quickly leave the bar and start walking down to the bottom of town. I feel an urgency to get as far away as I can before the sun really comes up and someone sees me.

It feels so exciting and scary all at once!

I get toward the bottom of town, and I see the stop for the bus.

And just as I get close to it, here comes the bus around the corner.

CHAPTER 12

——

The bus pulls up in front of me with a strong smell of diesel fuel and tires squeaking as it comes to a complete stop.

I hop on and try to find a seat. The bus is packed with people from other small towns farther south of us. I'm one of the last few stops before we get to Foggia, so there are only a few seats left. Nevertheless, I find a window seat near the middle. All the windows are open, but it still feels warm on the bus.

I have never been on a bus before, or to Foggia.

Even though I have an aunt and uncle who live there.

Watching the beautiful landscape as we drive by, I think about my aunt in Foggia. Zia Anna is my mother's half sister.

They have the same mother but two different fathers. She's married to a man named Mario, but he's in jail for stealing.

I asked my mother about them a few weeks before I left. Just out of curiosity. I wanted to know how they got to Foggia and where they live. She said her little sister was always a wild one and went for the wrong guys. She was hanging around with a guy named Mario Pizzo who had a bad reputation for drinking too much and starting fights. Anna couldn't wait to get out of Orsara, either, so she ran off with Mario and they moved to Foggia to get away from everyone.

Maybe I can stop over and have dinner with them sometime while I'm in school? I wrote their address down so I can visit them while I'm here. Oh, how exciting to finally be going to Foggia!

We wind around the small roads from Orsara to Troia. This is where Sylvia lives. It's such a cute town. Bigger than mine and the church is beautiful. I see people all around and I can't begin to imagine how many live here. Stores line the streets, and people look like they have more money than people in my town. We pass a small station on our way, and we stop to pick up two people while three get off.

We proceed down the hill and pass another church on the right and then a cemetery on the left. I see so many trees here, and the streets are much wider. I remember Sylvia said that she lives near the bottom of town. I wrote to Sylvia after the hospital, but I never heard anything from her. I wish I could get off and visit her, but now's not the time for that. I have to get to Foggia for school.

We continue down the road and onto a big highway heading northeast. It is wide open then. No homes, a couple of small factories and farms, but otherwise nothing until we get to Foggia.

As we pull into town, my mouth drops. This is the biggest town I've ever been to. It looks like what I think New York City would look like—tall buildings, lots of people, big streets and a bus station that is huge. I feel my stomach fluttering, and my heart is about to beat out of my chest.

As I get off the bus, I see someone with a uniform who looks like he works for the bus line. "Excuse me, sir, can you tell me how to get to Liceo Classico?" I can hardly contain myself and getting to the school is my top priority.

"Certainly, Signora." He proceeds to give me each left and right I need to walk to get there. But he assures me it's only a fifteen-minute walk, so I thank him and begin my journey.

As I walk through the streets of Foggia, the buildings amaze me; tall ones and short ones, and many seem to have offices in them where people can work. Some apartments, too, but mostly offices where I am. I pass a beautiful park, right smack in the middle of the city with lush, green trees and walkways, very different from my home, and suddenly I feel my nervousness start to come back to me.

With all the excitement of the bus and arriving in town, I forgot about my fear, but now that I am walking to school, I feel it again.

It isn't long before I get there, and boy, is it a sight to see! It's a beautiful university that looks almost like a church. I see people all around the building talking and looking happy. I feel excitement in the air, and I feel the pressure building in my chest. I walk around a bit to get the lay of the land, and I see a sign that says Registrazione.

Here I am!

Once inside, I go straight to the counter where a nicely dressed woman with glasses is sitting moving papers around.

"Good morning, I'm here to register for classes. My name is Claudia Valentino," I say nervously.

"Good morning, dear." The woman acknowledges me and begins rifling through her papers. She looks over her glasses up at me and asks my name again.

"Claudia Valentino. I'm here from Orsara. I just arrived by bus." I give her more information than she cares to hear.

She continues to look through her papers and finds what looks like a list. She runs her pointer finger down the list of names, scanning each one carefully, looking for my name. I see a look of confusion on her face, and she looks at me over her glasses again. "I don't see your name here, dear. When did you register?" she asks.

I start to sweat. Register? What exactly did that mean?

"I'm not sure what you mean. I'm here to sign up for school now," I say, a little worried.

"I'm sorry but you must register ahead of time and pay the fees. Have you paid the tuition?" she asks me, but I'm pretty sure she already knows the answer to her own question.

My shoulders slump down, I close my eyes, and I can feel the embarrassment showing in my face. I didn't know I had to register and pay ahead of time. I didn't do either.

I feel a sense of panic coming over me and my stomach is queasy.

"Well can I register now? And how much does it cost? I have some money now and can make arrangements to pay the rest." I'm quickly thinking that I can get a job while I'm in school to pay for the fees. I go through it all in my mind in a split second. Yes, I can definitely do this.

"No, I'm sorry we can't do that," the woman says carefully as I cut her off.

"Oh please, miss, can you check again? I must be able to start school. I can't go back to my town." I'm pleading for help.

"Our school is full right now, so you'll have to try again next year. Just remember to register ahead of time and pay the fees before you come." She is trying to be nice, but I'm crushed. My eyes start to water, and my emotions rush up, flooding my whole body with a sense of defeat.

What she just said doesn't make sense to me, and I walk away without even saying thank you or goodbye. I feel the disbelief come over me and the heaviness of this is weighing me down. I can barely walk.

I manage to shuffle my feet out the door and immediately the tears start rolling down my cheeks.

What am I supposed to do now?

I aimlessly walk around the streets for what feels like forever. This is the worst thing that has ever happened, and I didn't even see it coming.

How did I not know I had to register ahead of time?

No one ever mentioned it, and I suddenly feel very dumb. My emotions are getting the best of me, and I find a bench where I can sit and think. The tears are uncontrollable, and I feel helpless.

I sit for a long time, going through all of it in my head. I left my family this morning without even saying goodbye, and now I can't even go to school. I don't know how this happened or what to do next.

I finally pull myself together and open up my suitcase to get my aunt's address. I see a few people on the street to ask directions.

I arrive at her building where I find a list of names with buttons next to them on the door frame. I run my finger down the column of buttons until I reach the name Pizzo and push the button next to it. It makes an angry buzzing sound, and a woman's voice answers.

"Si?"

"Ciao Zia Anna, it's Claudia Valentino. Josefina's daughter?" I say trying to hold back my tears.

"Claudia!" She says with excitement. I've met her a few times over the years. She has come to town to visit us and help my mother, especially when a new baby would come into our world, but it's been a while since her last visit.

I admire how she left our town, even if her husband turned out to be a dud.

"What are you doing here? Wait, I'll come out!" She buzzes the door open so I can walk inside. The hallway is dark and cold. I look up a long staircase in front of me and see her open her door. She comes out and stands at the top of the stairs.

"Claudia, come up!" I start walking up the stairs, and as I get to the top, she grabs my suitcase. "Come on in!" She walks me inside, puts my suitcase down, and gives me a big hug. I totally let it all go and now I'm sobbing in her arms like a baby.

"Claudia what's wrong? What happened to you?" She asks.

I begin to tell her my story, and I can barely stop crying right there in the entrance of her little apartment. She listens and tries to console me, but I know it's hopeless. She doesn't have the money to give me for school, even if the registration wasn't closed.

"Listen, you just have different choices that you need to make now. You're out of school, so maybe you can stay here and help me a little. Foggia is a big city. Make some more money before you go back to Orsara," she says wanting to calm me down and give me hope.

Back to Orsara.

Those words hit me hard.

I look at her not knowing what to say.

"Come on into the kitchen. Let's make an espresso and talk some more." She walks toward the back of the apartment, and I follow.

The kitchen is small with a table and four chairs in the middle. Water runs into the sink, and against the wall stands a small stove with coils that turn orange with heat. She picks up the espresso pot and unscrews it. She fills the bottom half with water and coffee grinds and screws the top half back on. It clanks down onto the hot coil and then she grabs a tin from her cabinet.

"I made these myself, you know. Ricotta cookies. Have some." She pushes the tin in my direction. But I am too upset to eat anything right now.

She puts out two white saucers with small cups. Each cup gets a little silver spoon in it.

"You know you can't pour boiling hot liquid in a cup without having the spoon in it. It'll crack. Did you know that?" she asks. My thoughts are heavy and I'm hardly listening.

"What are you thinking, Claudia? What do you want to do now?" she asks me carefully.

"Zia, I don't know. I can't go back to Orsara like this. Besides, there's nothing there for me, but I don't know what I can do now. I have to wait a whole year before I can go to school." I start to whimper again at the thought of this.

"You know my sister Nadia lives in Chieri, and she told me there are a lot of job opportunities up there. She told your mother about them, too. I think she wants Josefina to move up there with her, but your mother won't do it right now. The kids are too small, you know." We look at each other in obvious agreement that my mother has too many babies.

"Maybe you can go north to Chieri?" she says.

North? I don't know a lot about Chieri, and I never thought of going north. Maybe I can get a job and go to school up there instead.

My aunt feels responsible for me, I can tell. She wants to make it better, and I really love her for that. I'm happy to be here with her even though I am crushed by the knowledge that I'll have to wait a whole year to go to school.

"Don't worry, Claudia. You can stay here with me for a little while if Chieri doesn't sound like a good idea. I'm sure we can find you a job so you can make some money to bring back to the family. The pay is pretty good if you know how to do domestic work." She knows how poor we are, and she also knows I know how to do that type of work.

My aunt wants me to help my family now since I can't go to school this year, anyway. Chieri might even be a better idea than staying here in Foggia. Maybe I need to go home and think it through again? My mother knows about Chieri so I can work that out with her, and I can probably keep working for the baker.

My thoughts are occupying my mind, and I'm quickly brought back to reality when my aunt speaks.

"Claudia, did you hear me?" Zia Anna asks.

"Yes Zia, and no, thank you. I have enough money for a bus ride home. I'm just going to go back and figure it out from there. I can't stay here. If I start working, I might never get back to school, and that would just break my heart," I say honestly.

I know of some kids who started working and bringing money home, and their parents didn't let them stop to go back to school. They got used to the money coming in and I don't want that to happen to me.

The espresso hisses, and the liquid starts to boil up into the top half of the pot. The hissing gets stronger and stronger until the top is full and boiling over a little. My aunt removes it from the heat and slowly pours the espresso into the cup over the spoon. It smells familiar, like home.

I take a sip of the hot liquid and feel my shoulders drop a little. I have to accept this setback, but I'm not giving up. I take a small bite of a cookie and know I will figure this out.

"By the way, how's Uncle Mario?" I want to change the subject, and she hasn't mentioned him since I've been here.

"That *bastardo*, he's in jail right now. *Stupido*." I already know this since my mother told me, but it's clear she doesn't think that I know about it.

"What did he do?" I ask.

She gets up and starts waving her hands around like she's shooing it away.

"He borrowed some tools from a job he was working on. He wanted to use them for another job since he didn't have his own, but instead of asking, he just took them. Stupido bastardo!" Now it seems like she wants to change the subject.

"What does your mother think about all this? I'm surprised you're here to tell you the truth." Zia Anna knows my mother needs my help. Letting me come to Foggia is a big deal.

"Well, I just left early this morning. I didn't want anyone to stop me. My mother knew I was saving for school, but I don't think she ever thought I would leave. I just had to get out of there," I say apologetically to my aunt. She gives me a look that says she completely understands and then sits back down at the table.

"Well let's go to the post office today and call back to Orsara. Your mother must be worried." I agree and start to clean up the table. Her home is lovely, and I can see myself living here with her for a little while, but I decide it's really not a good idea.

"Okay let's go." I'm feeling worn out and not up to making any more decisions. "Can I stay for a few days? Until I decide what to do?" I ask.

"Of course, you can. We'll have a nice dinner together tonight. We can stop at the market and pick up some fresh bread and mozzarella. I have nice tomatoes and basil already here." She takes command.

This all sounds wonderful to me. At least I can have one nice evening with my aunt and not worry too much about the future for now. We walk out of her apartment and down to the busy street. The post office is a short walk down the block and we ask to make a call. The post office in Orsara was the only place we could call to send word back to my mother quickly. We ask the postmaster to send a message to my mother that I'm okay, can't go to school, and I'll write her a letter once I figure out my plans. And to let her know that I'm with Zia Anna.

Once we finish at the post office, we walk to a market that is on the way back to her apartment. The market has such beautiful food on display, colorful vegetables of red and green. Pre-made pasta, which we only got to buy as a treat, was in abundance.

And the smells!

All those cheeses!

I love the smell of cheese and fresh bread. I didn't realize how hungry I was until I walked into that market.

I think I've been hungry most of my life.

I want to pay for something, just to show my aunt how much I appreciate her help, but she doesn't let me. We walk back to her apartment just catching up on all the family gossip we each know. She certainly seems to know more than I do, but I have a few tidbits to tell her, too.

Inside we lay out the bread and cheese, slice the tomatoes, and pour a couple of small glasses of red wine. I don't usually drink much wine, but tonight I feel like having some wine with my aunt.

We laugh a lot and enjoy our evening together.

But deep inside I feel the pain of defeat.

I make the most of this beautiful night, knowing that my time here is limited.

Soon I will be back in my little town, and suddenly my body starts to ache.

CHAPTER 13

———

The next morning, I am awakened by the sun coming in the bedroom window. I hear a faint sound of birds chirping outside and some church bells in the distance. It was the most comfortable night's sleep I've had since the hospital, and I slept hard.

As soon as my eyes open, I am up and out of bed. I wake up with a clarity that I wasn't expecting. I know what I need to do.

I put on the dress I took from Paola, and I'm ready to go. I meet my aunt in the kitchen.

"Buon giorno. How did you sleep, amore?" A fresh table-cloth covered in yellow squares, with colorful bouquets of flowers in the middle of each square, brightens the table. She puts out an espresso and a few more cookies.

"Bene, grazie. I got a good night's sleep. I think I needed it. I was exhausted last night." I sit down almost breathless at the thought of my day yesterday.

My aunt chuckles. "Well, you had a hard day and a little wine. I'm sure you were tired mentally more than anything. It was a big shock, you know, what you went through." She gives me a half smile and her face looks soft. For a moment

I think she kind of resembles my mother, only a prettier version of her. The years have been good to her, and it shows on her face. My mother's face shows a hard life.

"I know Zia, but I still feel like I got run over by a train," I say, wanting to share my clarity with her.

"You know, Zia Anna, I think Chieri just might be a good idea after all. I can't go back to Orsara. I'm afraid I'll never leave again if I do that. The more I think about it, it seems like I could make more money in the North to send home, anyway. I'm sure I can go to school there, too. And find a cheap place to live. You know?" I'm convincing myself as much as I'm trying to convince her.

"Well, it's worth a try, that is, if you're sure it's what you want? It's not going to be easy moving up North by yourself. I mean, my sister is there and I'm sure she will help you, but I don't know how much she can do." We drink our espressos quickly.

"I don't want anyone to give me anything! I'm willing to work. I want to work. I want to pay for my own things and go to school, too," I say firmly. I don't want my aunt to think I am looking for a handout. I just want to make my own money and make my own choices.

"Let's talk about it later. Come on, we'll be late for church." We finish the last drops of espresso and bites of ricotta cookies and clean up.

"It's okay," she says, trying to reassure me as we walk toward the front door. "I'm not saying that you want a handout. I know you're a hard worker and you're smart. I'm sure you'll be fine. I just don't want you to go to Chieri and not completely understand what it's like there." We pick up our sweaters and walk out the door.

"I know, Zia. I'm not expecting anything from Zia Nadia, but it'll be nice to have a family member close by. Someone

I can trust, you know? Maybe we can write her a letter, or is there a way to call?" Suddenly I'm feeling anxious, but hopeful about the prospect of some job opportunities up there for me.

"Of course, let's send a letter and let her know you're here in Foggia with me and want to move to Chieri. We'll ask her about where you can live and see what she says. In the meantime, you can get a job for the extra traveling money you'll need. Maybe you stay here for a few weeks until we hear back from Zia Nadia?" she says.

I think that sounds perfect! "Oh, Zia, I'm so happy!" I throw my arms around her and give her a big hug and kiss.

"Thank you, thank you for not making me leave just yet. I promise I won't be difficult, and I'll help you do all of your work around the house. I'm very good at sewing you know, if you need anything fixed." I'm excited to stay here in Foggia.

My aunt puts her arm around my waist and guides me to start walking toward the church. "That sounds like a great idea. I need a few things mended and tomorrow is Monday—we'll look for some work so you can start to put some extra money aside. You don't need to pay me for being at my house. Helping with the housework and doing some sewing for me is payment enough." She smiles and stops to give me a hug on the sidewalk. I am feeling very thankful, and church is where I need to be.

As we get closer to church, the bells are ringing and the birds are chirping. They seem to be in unison with each other, creating a beautiful, welcoming melody. We enter Chiesa di San Domenico and the scent of palm is all around. It's such a distinctive smell that reminds me of holidays. This church is one of the oldest buildings in town, right in the center, and the crowds are bustling about, looking for a place to sit and enjoy the mass.

It's a beautiful church, much bigger than my church at home, with rows and rows of brown wooden pews facing the altar. I look up to a domed ceiling that looks like a star—five spikes of light blue brilliance leading to a heavenly fresco of a cross in the center. It's like a beacon of hope for all the souls who sit below it.

I feel drawn to its energy, and I lose myself in its beauty.

I am so thankful to be going to church right now. I feel the need to thank God for the clarity I have and pray that I can get to Chieri and start working. We take our seats to the right of the altar, in the middle of the center aisle. Everyone is taking their seats and buzzing around with excitement that every Catholic understands. People are happy to see each other and appreciate having this place to meet and catch up on the happenings of the week. I need this right now.

The procession begins from the back, and we all stand to the music. The priest walks up the center aisle with his entourage of helpers, all dressed in beautiful robes that show authority. It's been a long time since I've enjoyed being in church this much.

The music stops and the mass begins. We sit, we stand, we kneel, but most importantly we listen. Listen to the message in today's mass. The priest talks about our strength, and how we find our strength in God. This message couldn't have come at a better time. Mass ends and I feel even more sure of my path. I am moving to the North.

I don't think I was this excited when I thought I was going to school here in Foggia. Going to the North is a much bigger idea, and it gets me closer to America.

That night we prepare the letter for Zia Nadia and I write down all the details of my dreams.

It amazes me to see it on paper.

The next morning, after we visit the post office, my aunt takes me around to a few shops near her apartment where she knows the owners. She asks if they need some temporary help and explains my plans. So far, we've tried four places but we're not having much luck. No one is looking for help right now, and I'm feeling discouraged

One of the last shops we go into is a tailor. *La Satoria.* Signor Sarto makes men's suits and needs some help with stitching. This is something I can do for sure.

"Signorina, let me see how you do a few stitches on this cloth." He says skeptically as he looks at my distorted hand.

I pick up the needle and thread it like a pro, just like I learned in sewing class back home. I quickly begin to do a backstitch, carefully going behind the fabric of the previous stitch. My fingers are small and even though my hand is deformed, I sew with ease. I do this for a few minutes then ask him what other stitches he wants to see me do. His mouth is slightly open, and he clears his throat and says no need. He hires me on the spot! It isn't a lot of money to start, but I am happy to be working.

I show up the next morning ready to work. The store is full of luxurious fabrics like wool and tweed. He also has some beautiful linen for warmer months. He cuts the fabric and pins the suits together on a mannequin. Then he instructs me on which sections are ready for basting. My favorite part is the finishing stitches, especially around the lapel of the suit coat. They require the most skill.

I spend all day basting and stitching and before I know it, the day is over. Signor Sarto is very pleased, and he says he will pay me at the end of the week.

I walk home tired, fingers sore.

The sounds of the town on my walk home are loud and full of opportunity. People walking and talking in the streets, making plans for the evening. Cars driving by, birds chirping. I can feel the excitement around me. Reminding me there is life outside of Orsara.

Every day I walk to and from work and think about my future, think about how far I can go. I don't even know how far I can go, but I feel the desire to try.

A week goes by and Signor Sarto tells me he's been very happy with my work. "Claudia, your work is amazing. You really have a natural gift. Won't you consider staying a bit longer than you thought, just to help me get through all my orders? I have so many people who are anxious to have their suits done, and I could really use you." He pleads.

I smile and let out a deep sigh. I really do appreciate that he likes my work and wants me to stay. But I don't want to tell him how I really feel. The truth is I can't wait to go to Chieri.

He sees my expression and starts again. "Yes, I know, you are moving North. But you can't blame me for trying." He grins and gives me an envelope with my pay for the week. I don't open it. I thank him very much, put it in my purse, and leave for the weekend.

When I get home, I go to my room and open my envelope. Signor Sarto actually paid me double what I thought he would pay. This is more money than I've ever made! A few weeks of this and I'll have more than enough money to go north.

A knock on my door startles me out of my amazement. "Come in," I say with a grin from ear to ear. I can hardly contain my excitement.

"I'm about to start dinner, do you want to come and help me? Afterward we can walk down and get a gelato. What do you think?"

I smile big. I would love an ice cream. "Yes, Zia, that sounds great, but only if it can be my treat." I flash her the envelope with all the money inside. I am feeling very proud now that I've gotten such a large pay. And besides, she's done so much for me, buying her an ice cream is the least I can do.

"My goodness, Claudia, you worked really hard this week. That's amazing! Make sure you put it in a safe place, and only carry a little money around with you at a time. You don't want to bring all that money out with you every day," she says authoritatively.

"Yes, Zia, I know. I'll just keep a little money in my purse, but the rest will stay here. I need to save as much as possible for my trip. Maybe I should open a bank account?" I think about the fact that my parents don't have a bank account.

"That's a good idea. It'll be safer there, and you really don't want to leave too much money lying around here. That bastardo Mario may be home soon. I think he's getting out of jail soon. He'll take every last penny you have if he finds it." Her face twists when she mentions his name.

Suddenly I panic. I can't bear the thought of working and being robbed again.

That's it—I'm opening a bank account.

My aunt and I prepare a nice dinner of pasta with white beans and olive oil, a tomato and cucumber salad, and some bread to dip into the salad juice. I chop up the vegetables and basil for the salad while she boils the water for the pasta and prepares the beans. She has some already prepared, so she just heats them in some olive oil and garlic before mixing them with the cooked pasta. She adds a ladle full of pasta water to the dish, and we sit to eat.

"Zia, I am so shocked at how much I got paid for this week's work. I never made that much before. You know, it makes me think if I work very hard, I can probably save enough money for my family to move, too. There's nothing in Orsara for them, and I don't want to leave my parents and sisters and brothers behind," I say genuinely.

"In the North, I can make enough money to send them all bus tickets. Do you think my mother would move?" I ask. I have seen in my mother's face that she wants something more for herself and her family, but I think she doesn't know how to get it. Especially with all those kids.

"You know, Claudia, I think if there was a way for her to move out of Orsara, she'd do it. You'll have to save a lot of money to move everyone, I know she won't go unless everyone goes. And maybe they can all get jobs in the North?" Zia Anna says.

Suddenly I miss my family and home. I have only been away for a little over a week, but I think of our little house and my sisters and brothers, and I feel a little pit in my stomach. I'm not going back, but I want to be with them, and I think this might be the way.

"You're right, Zia. I'm going to write my mother and let her know of my plans now that I think they could all come. I'll send her some money, too." Making all that money has given me hope that I will see my family all together again, and maybe they can have a better life, too.

After dinner we clean up and walk to get a gelato. It is a beautiful September evening, and my aunt shows me some of her favorite buildings in town. She has a thing for architecture and loves pointing out the places that she thinks are the most beautiful. She likes the newer buildings, but I love the antique ones.

Once we get back, my aunt goes to her room to read, and I go to write my mother that letter. I write all about my ideas.

I tell her there are jobs in the North and that they should consider moving up there, too. I tell her how I wrote a letter to Zia Nadia and as soon as I have more information, I'll send her another letter with details. I put half my pay inside, lick the envelope shut, and put it in my purse. I'll go to the post office first thing tomorrow.

I go to bed feeling happy and very excited to send my mother this letter.

———————

The next morning, I get up and go about my usual Saturday routine. I have some housework to do for my aunt and a little mending that she left for me on the kitchen table. I'm busy most of the morning. As soon as I finish, I run out to the post office to mail my letter, bringing my money with me so I can open a bank account.

At the post office, I purchase the stamp and hand my letter to the man behind the counter. I ask for my Aunt Anna's mail and take the letters back for her.

Next I go to the Banca D'Italia. The man at the desk opens an account for me and I give him my money to deposit. I start to worry about handing my money over to a stranger, but I know it's the right thing to do. He hands me a little book with the amount written in it and tells me to bring this little book with me every time I come to make a deposit. The feeling of independence coming from this little book is palpable.

When I get home, my aunt is there, and I give her the mail. I tell her about the letter to my mother and that I put a little money inside. I know that will make her happy, and I'm right. She smiles and tells me she's proud of me. I'm proud, too. It's nice to make your own money, and even nicer to share it.

As she looks through the letters, she picks one up and flashes it to me. "This is from Zia Nadia! Let's see what she has to say." She runs her finger along the flap and opens it. The paper is very thin, almost see-through, and there are two pages. She starts reading me the letter out loud.

Ciao Anna!

It was so great to hear from you, and I'm happy that Claudia wants to move to Chieri. I've been trying to convince her mother for years and she just won't listen.

That's interesting. She's been trying to convince my mother for years? I wonder why she never told me about it? I suddenly feel a little annoyed.

There are plenty of job opportunities here, but I know for sure of one that's available right away. I know of a woman who's looking for a girl to cook and clean for her. She will pay very well, and we can include living arrangements, at least until she makes enough money to find her own place. I told her that I have a family member who could do it and she's ready for Claudia to come as soon as she can. Write me again and let me know when exactly you can be here, and I'll arrange the job and place to stay.

Hope to see you soon my loves!

Nadia

This is great news! Immediately I want to write a letter back and tell her I'm coming as soon as possible. My aunt sees the excitement in my face and reminds me of my job with Signor Sarto.

"Claudia, this is good money. I think you should work for a little longer and then move north. You want to have enough money, just in case you get there and need to rent a room right away. It's better to have too much money than not enough, and you can't disappoint Signor Sarto," she says logically.

She makes sense. Besides, by the time we send a letter back it'll be another week anyway. I agree and we write a letter back with all the details and tell her I will be there in one month. I think that'll give me enough time to help Signor Sarto with his backed-up orders and make enough money to take with me. I run the letter back to the post office before they close.

That night I dream of the shoes Zia Lucia wore when she came to visit us from America. I picture myself in the dream wearing those beautiful, heeled shoes, walking around on the cobblestone streets of Chieri. It's a dream that makes me laugh.

I don't know what the streets of Chieri even look like, but I'm excited to find out.

CHAPTER 14

——

The next few weeks are predictable, and I feel settled. Even if it's temporary. I know as soon as I move to Chieri everything will change again. Knowing my day-to-day activities for the next few weeks puts me at ease.

I spend my days working for the tailor and my weekends working around the house. Signor Sarto really likes my work, and I'm helping him get caught up, so he pays me well. He knows I'm leaving soon, so I work very long hours; he's trying to get as much out of me as he can. It's a pleasant place to work and other than my fingers being sore, I don't mind it at all.

One day, Signor Sarto and I are working in the store together. I'm doing my usual stitching on some pending jobs and he's working with customers who came in to look at fabric for new suits. As soon as they leave, he tells me he wants to give me a gift.

"I'd like to make you a dress, Claudia. I don't usually make dresses, but I have for my wife in the past and she seems to like them. I want you to have a nice dress to travel with. I have a few bolts of fabric from dresses I made for my wife in the back. Please, take a look at them and pick one. I'll take your measurements and it'll be ready in time for your trip," he says very kindly.

I am so amazed at this lovely gift that I throw my arms around his neck to express my gratitude.

"Thank you so much, Signor Sarto. This is the nicest gift anyone has ever given me!" I am so excited to have a new dress of my own. I can't wait to go and look through the fabrics. We go to the back of the store, and he shows me all the bolts that I can chose from.

Each is prettier than the next, and I have trouble deciding which one to choose. I narrow it down to my two favorites and finally chose one that is a solid, pale blue. It's so elegant, and the fabric is soft with a little shine to it, just right for all occasions.

"Beautiful choice, Signorina Valentino!" He bows his head at me as if I'm a paying customer.

I am beaming with pride.

"I'll have it ready for you by your last day. It'll be beautiful!" he says confidently. He knows his work is unmatched, and I already can't wait to see it.

———

My last two weeks in Foggia, I begin to make my arrangements. I want to make sure I'm ready and avoid delays in my travel plans. I don't want to make that mistake again.

On Saturday morning, I go to the train station to figure out my journey. They tell me I can get a train to Torino, but then I'll have to get a bus to get to Chieri. I purchase both tickets and now and there's no turning back.

"Zia Anna?" I call with a slightly raised voice when I come back to the apartment.

I hear her rustling around in the kitchen and walk back that way. "Look at what I got!" I'm smiling and happy to show her proof of my changing life.

"Oh Claudia, I'm so happy for you, but I'm not happy for me." She says with a somewhat sad look. "It's been so nice having you here. Usually I'm all alone, but you being here has been a pleasure. And you've really taken care of me, too," she says thankfully.

"Oh Zia, I'm sad to be leaving, too, but I must go. I know you understand, and I'll always be grateful for you helping me when I really needed it." I show her my tickets, and we plan our last week together.

She tells me she's going to take me to a place in the city where she says the food is good and we can have a celebratory dinner. She's so proud of me and says she knows I'll be fine.

But I'm a little worried. I don't tell my aunt this, but the many unknowns are scaring me. The excitement pushes the feelings of fear on the back burner, and I can't think of anything other than getting on that train next week.

"Guess what, Zia? Signor Sarto told me he's going to make me a dress for my trip," I say with a big smile. "He let me choose from leftover fabric he has from dresses he made his wife. I'd like to get a new pair of shoes to go with my dress. Can you come with me?" I ask.

"Of course, I'll go with you! And wow, that's so nice that he's making you such a special gift! I know he really appreciates all the help you've been lately. We can go today. Come on, I know a great store and it's not too far." She goes to grabs her purse and we walk out to the street.

We walk for about twenty minutes to an area in town with many shops. Coat stores, dress stores, places to buy stockings and makeup, and then finally a shoe store. The store is lined with shelves from floor to ceiling holding so many pairs of shoes, all different styles and colors. All beautiful in their own right!

Even though I have a specific shoe in mind, I enjoy walking around the store and looking at all the beautiful choices. I imagine all these different shoes and where I would go wearing each one. Saddle shoes, stilettos, kitten heels, flatties, all waiting for someone to buy them. All waiting for their lives to begin.

We take our time and look around. So many beautiful options, but I have a specific pair in mind. Simple high heels in black. A very classic shoe just like Zia Lucia had when she came to visit. Just like American girls wear.

A pair catches my eye and I stop to pick it up. A black pump, not too high but not too low, with a small bow in the front. Black leather. Classic and simple. The perfect shoe for my new life.

"Zia, what do you think?" She's walking around admiring at all the shoes, too.

"I think they're perfect Claudia!" She says with approval.

The salesman measures my foot and brings me a pair in my size to try. As I slip them on and walk around, I feel like a movie star. I have a little trouble walking in the high heel, but I'm amazed at how quickly I pick it up. They are so soft and feel like they are wrapped around my foot. It's like nothing I've ever felt before.

"They're just right!" I say in excitement, as I still wobble around a bit, thinking I'd better practice wearing these around the house before my trip.

I take them off and hand them to the salesman, who puts them nicely back in the box. Even the packaging is beautiful.

We spend the rest of the afternoon visiting the other shops in town. We see so many beautiful things, but I can't afford to spend money on anything else. Just the shoes for now.

"Zia Anna, I'm sorry that I've spent so much time preparing for my trip that I didn't get my weekend chores done," I say.

"Non ti preoccupare. Don't worry yourself," she says sweetly.

"Well still, let's get back so I can do them before bed. I can finish the rest after church tomorrow," I say, determined. I want to get as much done as I can before my last week here in town. My train to Torino leaves next Saturday morning, and I have to work all week. I want to make sure I leave Zia Anna's house in good shape before my move. It's the least I can do for her.

"Okay let's go. We'll pick up a little something for dinner on our way," my aunt says.

———

Around midweek, I go into work and Signor Sarto is excited to show me the dress.

"Claudia, what do you think? This is it here, the one I made for you," he says as his hand floats gracefully toward the mannequin wearing my new dress. He's beaming with pride, rightfully so. It truly is the most beautiful dress I've ever seen.

It has shirt buttons on the front, pleats at the shoulders, and a rounded collar. It is very fitted around the waist with a wide skirt that comes down probably to the middle of my calf.

"Oh Signor Sarto, I can't believe what you've done. This is so amazing, beyond words!" I exclaim. I can't wait to try it on.

"I have a little surprise for you." He goes behind his table and pulls out another dress. "Try this one on. I made you two since I had enough fabric. They're both the same style since it was the only way I could make two so quickly. But I didn't think you'd mind that, and I know you had such a hard time picking just one," he says as he hands me the second dress of pale green.

My heart is jumping out of my chest! Two dresses? How could I possibly have two beautiful dresses of my own, brand new and just for me? I am more excited than I've ever been.

"Come on, let's go. I want to see if I need to make any adjustments before your last day on Friday." He removes the blue dress from the mannequin and hands it to me. I go to the back and try it on.

"Signor Sarto, I think it fits just right!" I walk out twirling around in my new dress so he can see.

"No, I see a few small adjustments I want to make. I can't let you walk around Chieri like this!" He picks up some pins and puts them in a couple of places. I quickly change and he does the same to the green dress.

"Okay," he says, "go change." He reminds me not to disturb the pins. "I'll fix them both tonight."

"Oh, thank you so much, Signor Sarto. This is the nicest gift I've ever received in my whole life." I hug him again, grateful that I have these two beautiful dresses, but also grateful for the opportunity he gave me over the last several weeks.

"You're welcome, Claudia. You've been a pleasure to have in my store. I hope I will see you again someday." But I think he knows he probably won't.

I can leave Foggia feeling content. I helped Signor Sarto get caught up with his orders, and I saved enough money to help with my move. Everything is falling into place.

The end of the week arrives, and Signor Sarto has put the finishing touches on my dresses.

"Oh, Signor Sarto, these dresses are incredible!" I say as he proudly shows me his work. "I will feel like a princess wearing them!" I am giddy with excitement at the sight of these beautiful dresses.

"It was my pleasure to make them for you, and I'm happy you like them," he says with satisfaction.

They truly are the most beautiful pieces of clothing I've ever owned. I couldn't thank him enough for putting in the time to make them for me.

I give him a big hug. "Thank you so much for everything, Signor Sarto. Not only for the dresses, but also for the opportunity to work with you. I really appreciate it, and I will miss you and your store very much," I say sincerely.

"I will miss you, too, Claudia. You have always been a ray of sunshine in my store, and it will be dark without you," he says sweetly, and bows his head. I see a tear in his eye, and it reminds me of my father when he left me at the hospital.

It's a bittersweet goodbye, and I leave his store content and ready for what's to come.

CHAPTER 15

———

I put on the new pale blue dress that Signor Sarto made for me with my new black pumps.

I brush my hair out and pull it up in a low bun.

I feel beautiful.

Friday night! It's my last night in Foggia, and my aunt has something special planned. She wants me to experience a fancy dinner before I leave, so we're going to a very nice restaurant to celebrate.

I walk out of my room to tell my aunt I'm ready to go, and I see her in the kitchen, wearing a pretty, red dress and ready for our night out.

"Wow, Claudia, that dress fits like a glove! I've never seen anyone look so beautiful!" she says with excitement.

"Thank you, Zia. And I love your dress too!" I say. "This whole experience has been one that I'll never forget. Coming to Foggia was supposed to be my way to go to school, and then when that didn't work out, I really thought I was going to have to go back to Orsara." I let out a deep breath.

"The thought of that really scared me Zia. But you helped me through that bad time, and now I'm really excited to go to Chieri!" I express my gratitude honestly to my aunt.

"Well, I understand that you're excited, but Claudia, please remember to be careful. You're going to a whole different part of Italy. Things are different in the North. People are different and things move faster than you've been used to in the South. You may feel a little out of place. But don't let that slow you down." She winks at me and continues.

"Just remember where you're from and always make sure you can hold your head up high. You just do your best, and I'm sure everything will work out." She comforts me with her words.

I feel a little funny. Worried about what she just said. What did she mean that I may feel a little out of place? How different could things be?

"Come on, let's go. We're going to be late for our dinner." She picks up her purse and we leave for our night out. It is a mild night, and everything is beautiful at the restaurant. It is a beautiful end to my stay with Zia Anna.

That night when we get back from dinner, I write a letter to my mother and Paola. I want them to know my plans and that I'll be with Zia Nadia in Chieri. I tell them to write me there and let me know how everyone is doing back home.

I hope they will make plans to come and see me.

I get it all ready and ask my aunt to bring it to the post office tomorrow.

Everything is done, and I am finally ready for my trip!

The next morning, I pack the last few things I have out in my small suitcase and say my goodbyes to my aunt. She has tears in her eyes and so do I. But we're not letting it get the best of us. I have a train to catch so there's no time to waste.

The train leaves precisely at 8:00 a.m. It's about a nine-hour ride, so I pack a few taralli biscuits, nuts, and an orange to snack on. I also pack my small booklet, pencil, and a handkerchief in my purse.

We hug one last time and hold on for longer than usual. She gives me a kiss on my cheek, and I leave.

As I walk to the station, I take very deep breaths of the crisp morning air, trying to soak in every last bit of Foggia. It's been so damp lately, but not today. This pleasant fall morning is good to me, and my excitement is building with every step I take.

"Ciao signore." I show my ticket to the gentleman at the station. "Please tell me where I need to go to catch my train to Torino." I ask politely.

"Certainly, Signora. You can walk through those doors to the main platform to get to the train. It's already here so don't waste any time." He points to his right to direct me as I take my ticket back and make my way over to the doors.

The station is loud, and the ceilings are high and a strong smell of cigarette smoke surrounds me. I walk through the doors and onto the platform to the dark and shadowy presence of the train. It is a spectacle! I don't know how many cars there are, but it seems to stretch on forever. The engines are deafening, and the smell of fuel is burning my nose. But that doesn't stop me from seeing this train as a forceful energy, pushing me to grow in ways I never thought I could.

It is magnificent, and I am like an adventurer about to embark on an exciting journey.

I walk onto the train with my suitcase, and a gentleman in a dark blue uniform and cap greets me.

"Ciao signora. Let me see your ticket, please," he says in a gentle voice. I hand him my ticket, and he directs me where to go. "Have a nice trip, signora!"

I walk down the aisle with rows of windows to the left of me and roomettes to the right. Each roomette has six seats and a big picture window so you can watch the landscape as you travel. As soon as I reach mine, I go inside, put my suitcase on the rack above my seat, and plop down. All my nervousness is rising up in my throat, and I feel my emotions taking over.

Lots of people are starting to come onto the train; I see them walking past my door. Women, men, children. All clean, hair combed, nice clothes. I'm amazed at the life that exists outside of my small town, and I start to think about home.

I wonder what everyone is doing right now. I picture my mother making dough for the pasta, Paola is probably taking care of the younger ones. One of my brothers is getting water. My father may be fixing pot handles or rolling cigarettes. I'm sure everyone is busy, and I wonder if they are thinking about me, too.

The door to my room opens and a couple walks in.

"Ciao," they say, smiling. They're older than me, but not by much. They're holding hands, and the gentleman gives the woman a kiss before she sits. I wonder where they're final destination is? Everyone on the train is on their own adventure, and we're not all going to the same place. I'm fascinated by that.

"Ciao. How are you?" I say politely.

"Bene grazie, it's a beautiful train, isn't it?" the gentleman says.

It really is. The seats are a beautiful brown leather, and everything looks very new, and smells new, too. Curtains hang in the windows, and the ash trays are clean enough to eat out of. Artistic representations of Italian countryside and cityscapes are built in above the seats. I think Paola would love this.

The couple takes their seats and are very excited to talk to each other. The door opens again, and a woman comes in with a child. She looks to be about my mother's age and the little boy is about ten years old. He is wearing a wool suit and a cap and follows his mother courteously. They take their seats and smile at all of us in the room.

The train is filling up as we approach our departure time. I settle into my seat and close my eyes. The sounds and smells are a lot to take in. I feel comfortable and content and feel like I need to write down my thoughts.

I take out my little booklet that I got from my last America package. I'm happy I brought it with me so I can write down all my experiences. I'm seeing so many new things and, I'm afraid if I don't write them down I might forget.

I write about the train and the passengers that I'm sharing the roomette with. The little boy reminds me of my brothers. I watch him sitting quietly, swinging his legs as his mother gives him something to eat.

I write about my feelings, both good and bad. I'm so engrossed in what I'm doing that I don't even realize the train has started moving out of the station. It isn't until we pick up speed in the countryside that I lift my eyes from the pages of my booklet to look outside.

The train is moving so fast, and outside I can see rolling hills of grain speeding past me. A few trees are in the landscape, but mostly fields. The long strands of grain sway gently back and forth in the gentle breeze, like a peaceful dance.

I close my book and begin wondering about where my travel companions are going. The mother with her son have both fallen asleep, so I strike up a conversation with the young couple first.

"Where are you traveling to?" I say, hoping they aren't offended that I ask. They look at me with friendly smiles and begin to speak excitedly about their trip.

"Well, we just got married and now we're going on our honeymoon in Rapallo. We're taking the train to Torino first to visit my aunt," the woman says. She's very pretty and has a beautiful suit and hat on.

"She's very old, and I'm afraid if I don't stop to see her now, when we're in the North, we might not get the chance. We'll visit with her for a few days, and then we'll go to Rapallo for the rest of the trip. How about you? Where are you going?" she says, turning the attention to me.

I'm very excited to tell my story. I fill them in on my big move from Orsara to Chieri and how I have a job there waiting for me. Leaving a little town in the South to go to the North is a big deal, at least for me it is.

We continue with the small talk for a little while until we run out of things to say. The husband doesn't say anything, he just listens. He gets up and leaves our room to check out the rest of the train, the wife closes her eyes and takes a nap, and I continue to be amazed at the beauty around me. Right now, it's a lot of fields, but I'm excited to see more life as we get farther north.

"Where are you going?" I hear a whisper of a sweet voice ask. The little boy has awakened and is being careful not to wake his mother.

"I'm going to Chieri. I have a job there waiting for me," I whisper back. "What about you? Do you know where you're going?"

"Of course, I know. We're going to Lake Orta. I have a break from school, so we're going to visit my mother's sister and her family. I'm going to fish when I'm there," he states.

"Fish? Really? Fish for what?" I ask curiously. I wonder how much this seemingly smart little boy knows about fishing.

"Perch. We can't eat them since the water isn't good, but we can still catch them. I like fishing." He smiles as he says this.

"Well, that sounds like a wonderful adventure. I hope you catch lots of perch!" I say excitedly and turn back to my view. I find comfort in his smile. It's innocent and peaceful, and he calms my nerves a bit.

The train makes a few stops along the way, dropping some people off, picking some people up. I'm in for a long ride, so I just sit patiently and wait in between each stop. I pass the time looking out the window, fidgeting with excitement as I get closer to Torino.

———

Several hours have gone by and I start to see names of towns that are familiar. Rimini, Bologna, Milan, each one with its own picture in my mind. We approach Torino and I see more people gathered at the station than in all of Foggia.

Torino is a big city, and the station is evidence of that; lots of people waiting on platforms with luggage and kids, all with exciting lives and places to go. At least that's how it seems to me.

The train begins to slow down as we reach the tight quarters of the platform and eventually it comes to a stop in Porto Nuova Station. My heart is jumping out of my chest. I still have a bus to catch before I see my aunt, and in her last letter she said she'd meet me at the station in Chieri. I wonder if she'll recognize me. I haven't seen her since I was very little and with my new dress and shoes, I hardly look like I did back then.

I get my bag down from the overhead rack, pick up my purse, and walk out of the roomette. Everyone is filing out at the same time, so I wait in line behind others to get off the train.

Eventually I step down onto the platform and feel some relief.

I walk toward the doors to escape the noisiness of the train, then up the stairs to the station. It's very ornate, an incredible sight to see of red walls and arched ceilings. It feels over-embellished for a train station. I stop at the information booth to ask where I can catch my bus to Chieri; they direct me outside.

The sights are amazing out on the street. People, cars, buses, all around. The hustle and bustle on a Saturday night is incredible. I can feel the heartbeat of the city, and suddenly I know for sure that this was the right move for me.

The bus ride to Chieri is easy and quick. Chieri is small, smaller than Foggia, and not what I expected. I'm already missing the hustle and bustle of the big city I arrived in by train.

"Claudia!" I faintly hear a voice calling me, but I'm not sure where it's coming from.

"Claudia, qui, I'm here!" It was Zia Nadia.

I turn in her direction and begin to walk very fast, almost a run. I run into her arms, drop my bags, and give her a big hug.

"Zia, how did you recognize me?" I ask very curiously.

"Gioia, sweet girl, you look just like your Zia Anna. I recognized you right away." That is a nice compliment. Zia Anna is the prettiest of my aunts. And I love that she calls me Joy. It's such a happy nickname.

"Oh, Zia, I'm so happy to be here. I was so nervous for the trip and afraid I wouldn't make it and here I am."

"Oh, I tell Zia Anna all the time that she should leave that bastardo jailbird of a husband behind and move up here with me. Your parents, too. Why didn't they come?" she asks.

I know why they didn't come. For a split second I feel embarrassed, but it's my aunt.

"Ahh, Zia, you know how it is in the South. They're always just trying to survive in Orsara. There's not enough work, so they do what they can to just keep moving forward. I couldn't stand that kind of life anymore. I want to go to school and get an education." I feel a little bad talking about my family.

"Ah I know how your mother is. She doesn't like to change very much. But you certainly didn't take after her, now did you? I'm so glad you're here. I have a great job ready for you, and we can talk all about it when we get home. Come on, pick up your stuff, let's go. We can get a taxi to my house," she says, leading the way.

I do as she says, and we walk out of the station. When we get outside, the streets are much quieter than Torino. This town isn't even as big as Foggia, and now I'm feeling skeptical. Torino is only a short bus ride away, though—at least that's what I tell myself. Regardless, I'm happy to be in the North.

It's a quick ride in the taxi, and as we pull up to Zia Nadia's home, a wave of happiness comes over me. It's a cute two-story house on a quiet, spacious cobblestone street. She has pretty vases full of greenery around the front door. It's modest, but much bigger than my home in Orsara.

"Zia, this is incredible. How long have you lived here?" I ask respectfully.

"Oh, we've been here a long time. Probably about ten years or so. Come on, let's go inside." She leads the way.

Zia Nadia's home looks comfortable. Spacious with tall windows looking out onto the street in the front of the house, and the garden in the back of the house. I can see why everyone in the South thinks the people in the North have it better. It's because they do.

Life in Orsara is simple, and there's a lot to appreciate about that. It's the town that taught me how to survive and be humble. But nothing compares to what I'm already seeing in the North. Between the hustle and bustle of Torino, and the quietly abundant life here in Chieri, I know I've seen too much.

I can never go back to Orsara again.

My uncle Marco comes out from the kitchen as soon as he hears us.

"Claudia, my goodness you've grown so big. How old are you now?" He gives me a hug as my aunt walks back to the kitchen.

"I'm seventeen, Zio. I'll be eighteen soon, and thank you so much for letting me stay here until I find a place to live." I take off my jacket and put it down on top of my suitcase. I'm already planning to look for a place to rent as soon as possible.

"Don't preoccupy yourself with that. You can stay here as long as necessary. Besides, I don't think Zia Nadia will let you leave." He's whispering now so my aunt won't hear him. He gives me a smirk and we both start laughing. My aunt is known to be a little bossy and possessive. Very different from Zia Anna. More like my mother.

I grab his hands and give him a very confident look. "It's okay, Zio. I'm happy to stay a little while. Besides it'll give me a chance to get some money together, but I have plans to move out and Zia Nadia knows this." I assure him that I won't be a burden.

"Well, you certainly are mature, aren't you? I'm glad you're here. Let's move your bag upstairs. I'm sure you're tired and want to rest a little before dinner. Your room is up here, come with me." Zio Marco carries my suitcase up and puts it down on the tiled floor of my room.

It's a lovely room with white linens on the bed and sheer curtains on the window that are blowing around with the night air. I can hear people chatting in the street and kids laughing. It's chilly in the room, but it feels fresh and comfortable.

I kick off my shoes and lay my head down on the pillow.

Instantly I feel relaxed and let out a long sigh.

I close my eyes and fall into a deep, deep sleep.

CHAPTER 16

———

I wake up to the sunlight peeking through my window. It warms the room and produces a lovely glow that makes me smile. The sheer white curtains are not moving anymore, and I have a blanket on top of me. I'm still wearing the dress I arrived in.

I pop up out of bed feeling like I was late for school. I suddenly feel bad that I fell asleep and didn't catch up with my aunt and uncle. I missed dinner, too, and now my stomach is grumbling.

"Claudia, are you up?" I hear my aunt coming in.

"Zia, I'm so sorry. I guess I was exhausted from my trip. Why didn't you wake me up? I didn't mean to be so rude," I say as I get up out of bed, put my hair in a low bun, and adjust my dress.

"Don't be silly, Gioia. You were tired, you should sleep if you need to. You just traveled a long distance, and I'm sure you could hardly sleep on that train. I saw that you fell asleep, so I closed your window and covered you up. It was chilly last night," she says, reassuring me.

And she was right. I was tired. She's taken the train back and forth from the South a few times, so she knows it's not the most comfortable trip. I may have closed my eyes for part of it, but I would hardly call it sleeping. Besides, I was too excited to sleep.

"Thank you, Zia. What can I do to help you today? I just need to change, but I'm ready to do whatever needs to be done." I say anxiously.

"We're going to go to church first. Then we can come home and make some fresh pasta for dinner. Wouldn't that be a treat?" she says with a big smile.

I don't have the heart to tell her that fresh pasta was hardly a treat, so I shake my head in agreement and put on the light green dress Signor Sarto made for me.

The church is very nice, and the bells sound like none I've ever heard before. But church bells all sound different. One thing I've noticed in the little bit of traveling I've done over the last few months is that mass is the same everywhere. I find it pleasant and comforting to know that every church follows the same routine. It's easy to be in sync with all the other people in the church no matter where you are. Everyone knows how to stand, sit, kneel, and do the sign of the cross whether you're in the North or the South.

On our walk back home, I ask Zia Nadia about the job.

"Zia, when can I start working? What is the job exactly?" I'm curious to know what I'm going to be doing while I'm here.

"Tomorrow, Gioia, I'll take you to meet Signora Marino. She's the woman who needs full-time help in her home. Cooking, cleaning, sewing, you know those things. I think she'll like you," my aunt smiles and says confidently.

I know I can do the job, and I'm anxious to start working. "Grazie, Zia, for setting this up for me," I say gratefully.

"You will do a good job. This I know for sure." She nods her head as she says it.

I hope I do a good job. I know how to do those things, but what if it's not the way the lady of the house wants it done? I guess I can't worry about that now. We have some fresh pasta to make.

Dinner is lovely, and we finish with an espresso, as usual. I retreat to my room to write in my notebook and to write two letters, one to Zia Anna and one to my mother. I need to let them know I've arrived and I'm okay.

I'm still tired so I go to bed early. Tomorrow will be another busy day.

In the morning, I awaken to a light rain, and I can hear it tapping against the roof of the house. I get up and get ready to meet my new employer.

Downstairs, my aunt and uncle are already having colazione. The kitchen is full of delicious smells of bread toasting and espresso brewing. The coffee pot hisses for attention, and my aunt takes it off the stove. She spreads a little butter and fresh raspberry jam on a piece of toast for me.

"Buon giorno," I say, happy to sit at the table and eat this beautiful breakfast. Growing up poor, you don't get things like butter and jam. Just the bread, and sometimes you have to cut the mold off before you eat it.

"Buon giorno, Claudia. How did you sleep?" my uncle asks.

"So good, Zio. Thank you. I—"

My aunt interrupts. "Are you ready for your day? You should put on a modest dress, and I have a white apron that would work. Make sure your nails are clean and trim, too. No one wants a girl with dirty fingernails cooking their food," she says matter-of-factly.

"I know, Zia. I will go trim them a little more before we leave. I have to stop at the post office, too. How long do I have?" I ask as I devour the toast and jam.

"Let's leave in about fifteen minutes," my aunt says as she hurries to clean up the kitchen.

I finish up my breakfast and head back to my room to change into the dress I took from Paola. It's not as nice as the ones Signor Sarto made, so it'll work well for a domestic job. It only takes me a couple of minutes and I'm back downstairs ready to go. The rain has stopped, and now the sun is peaking out, and I can see it coming through the windows in the back of the house.

I gather my jacket and the apron my aunt gave me, and we leave together. The cold air is piercing through me, and I realize the climate here will take some getting used to. After the post office, we walk down wide cobblestone streets that are no doubt beautiful when the flowers come out in the spring. Zia points out her friends' houses, the street to turn on for the little market, and a cute little garden in the middle of town that's seen better days.

She talks a lot, but I welcome it. I don't feel like talking since I have so much on my mind. I hope Signora Marino likes me.

We walk up to a very large, yellow home with a dark wooden door and a small balcony above it. I imagine a beautiful woman hanging over to see her visitors below. Gray shutters cover all the windows that are closed. The stone walkway is very smooth, with little bits of grass growing in between.

My aunt knocks on the door, and within a few seconds a woman answers.

"Ciao, Signora Marino, this is my niece Claudia that I told you about. She's here to help you with your housework." My aunt nudges me gently in front, and I reach out my hand to greet the woman. She has shoulder-length, wavy brown hair, and she's wearing a very pretty dark-blue dress. She doesn't look like she would clean her own house.

"Ciao Signora. It's a pleasure to meet you," I say as she shakes my hand and reciprocates the greeting.

"Thank you so much for coming today. I've been anticipating your arrival for some time. I really need help since my other woman left suddenly to tend to her sick husband. I'm sorry, but everything is in shambles and I have a lot of work for you to do right away. Can you start today?" She seems flustered and a little breathless when she speaks. And she's rambling on and on.

"Ah sure. Certainly, I can help you today. Zia, you can go home. I remember the way back. I'll stay and work for Signora Marino." I'm happy she wants me to start so soon. I guess I didn't have to worry about her liking me. I think she would've liked anyone who knocked on her door ready to work today.

"Okay, Claudia, but come right home when you're done. We'll wait for you for dinner." My aunt kisses my cheek and leaves.

"Okay, let's get started. There's so much to do and not a lot of time!" Signora Marino commands.

She starts walking through the house, showing me around and describing each room. I follow her, trying to pay attention to what she's saying while I'm looking around at everything. The floors are a beautiful burnt-orange tile, and all the walls are creamy white and smooth. Dark furniture pieces fill each room, and she has beautiful gold lighting throughout the house. She has pictures of family in ornate frames and vases with flowers in them. The kitchen is airy and bright with lots of room to work.

This might be a bigger job than I was anticipating.

"The cleaning supplies are out here," she says as we walk outside to a beautiful veranda covered with grapevines and overlooking a small garden. A long table with chairs, and overflowing pots of dying flowers and greenery stand in the middle. It's the end of the season, and there is a lot to clean up outside. A man tending to the pots barely notices us.

"We have another closet upstairs with more cleaning supplies so you don't have to carry everything up and down. We should have enough rags and buckets and brooms, as well. I like the house to be dusted and swept first thing every day when you come. Then you can spend the afternoon tending to the other chores and preparing the evening meal." She is speaking very fast and is very excited.

"Today just focus on cleaning," she says as she waves her hand in the air. "I'll take care of the cooking. Okay?" She hands me the broom, and I smile and tell her not to worry.

The house is very large but manageable. I begin in the front of the house and work my way back, dusting every tabletop and crevice. The dark wood furniture has so many twists and turns, it's a lot of work to get the dust out of it all. But I figure out how to use the rags and the duster to do the job right.

Every picture, trinket, vase, I handle all with care to remove any signs of neglect. The last thing I do is sweep the floors, and then I make my way upstairs.

The five bedrooms are beautiful, each one larger than the next, all with dark, wood exposed beams on the ceilings and tile on the floors. The windows in each room are as tall as I am with deep sills. I can see myself getting lost for hours sitting in one of these windows, just watching what's happening outside. Quietly, alone and peaceful.

I'm not even sure how many people live here or if they have children. But either way, I get the job done upstairs and go down to find the lady of the house.

"Signora." I call out, hoping she responds quickly. "I've finished the cleaning."

"Oh, Claudia that's great! Come in the kitchen and help me with the laundry please. Do you know how to iron?" she asks. I did a little ironing when I worked for Signor Sarto, but not much.

"A little bit, but I'm not that experienced at it," I say as I follow her back to the kitchen.

"It's okay. I'll show you the way I like it done to start. It's easy, anyone can do it." She picks up the iron and shows me very quickly how to use it and then hands it to me. It's clear that she doesn't want to be bothered with this job.

As I'm ironing, she's just chatting away. I am respectful and try to listen while I work.

"I grew up in this town, did you know that? Where did you grow up?" she asks with curiosity.

"I grew up in Orsara," I say quietly. I never want to talk about myself let alone where I grew up.

Her head tilts to one side and her eyes squint. "Hmm, I don't know that town. Where is that?"

"It's a small town in Puglia, near Foggia. Do you know Foggia?" I'm keeping my eyes on my ironing, so I don't burn the clothing and so I don't have to see her expression when she learns I'm from a small town in the South.

"Oh, yes, I know Foggia. That's a lovely town. I visited once when I was young. My mother had a friend who moved there. But I've never heard of your town. Oh well, nevertheless, I've spent my whole life here in Chieri, and now my husband works for the United States Consulate, so we entertain a lot.

We have visitors from out of town who will come and have dinner or even stay for a night or two. It's good we have all these extra bedrooms," she tells me.

Her posture changes ever so slightly and her shoulders drop. "We don't have any children, it just never happened for us," she says sadly.

"Well, you have a beautiful home, Signora, and I'm sure your guests really enjoy coming here," I say.

I know I'm already enjoying it here. It's a house I can only ever dream to live in. But I can't get my mind off her husband working for the Consulate. Zia Lucia filled out our applications for America as a family, but I never heard any more about it from her. Besides, my family isn't anywhere near ready to go.

But maybe he can help me figure out how to do it?

I get the ironing done, and it's close to the end of the day. She thanks me up and down and says to please come back tomorrow morning by 8:30 a.m. Then she'll go over everything we didn't cover today.

I thank her and leave, tired and hungry for dinner with my aunt and uncle.

CHAPTER 17

———

The next morning, I get up and get out the door early. I don't want to be even one minute late. In fact, I was five minutes early, hoping I would get to meet Signor Marino.

Signora Marino is even happier to see me today.

She opens the door with such enthusiasm that I think the handle almost breaks off.

And she's breathless again.

"Oh Claudia, I'm so glad you're here. We have even more to do today," she says.

I follow her inside, wondering what's in store for today.

"We have a guest coming to stay. My husband's brother is coming by boat from America. He arrives in Genoa today, so I want you to make sure his room is ready." She rattles off the details.

Genoa. Boat from America. I start daydreaming about going to America on a boat and what that must be like. Would it be like the train ride? There must be beds for sleeping since it's certainly a very long trip.

"Claudia, are you listening to me?" Signora Marino asks, and I'm quickly forced back into reality.

"Yes, of course, let's get started," I say quickly.

Today is much the same as yesterday with the list of my tasks, but I continue to learn more. She spends some time showing me how she likes her meals prepared. Different from what I'm used to in my house. She has spices and herbs and so many other ingredients to work with.

"Claudia, do you mind staying a little longer today? I could use the extra help until the men arrive. I'd like to set a nice table, and we should iron the tablecloth and napkins. Also, the sheets in the guest room need to be ironed. Did you notice that?" she asks as she recites the list of chores with ease.

"Certainly, Signora. No problem, I don't have anything that I need to do after work today so I can stay as long as you need me," I say, excited to meet Signor Marino and his brother.

I have been learning to cook with butter and garlic, olive oil, and pasta bought from the store. But today I'm making fresh pasta for her, my specialty, and she's very appreciative.

The day passes quickly. I have been so busy getting ready for dinner that I didn't even hear the front door open or Signor Marino come into the kitchen.

"Profuma delizioso!" He seems happy with the smells in the kitchen. I turn to see a very handsome, tall man who looks exactly as I pictured him. His brother is standing somewhat behind him, and both men are dressed in beautifully tailored suits. The brother is holding a suitcase.

"Ciao Signore. I am Claudia Valentino. I just started working here yesterday." I explain.

"Yes, I heard all about you last night. You must do very good work or my wife wouldn't have let you back in the house today." He turns to his brother and they both start to laugh.

"Oh but, forgive me for my rudeness. This is my brother Roberto," Signor Marino quickly says.

"Piacere," he says as he tips his head. He has a calm air about him.

I continue making the pasta as I think about Roberto. Why did he go to America and then come back? Is he going back anytime soon?

"It's a pleasure to meet you, Roberto. I know you are just returning from America, and I would love to hear about your trip. I have a couple of aunts who live there, and I'd like to go visit myself someday very soon." I feel very worldly as I share my plans.

"Oh, where in America are your aunts?" he asks curiously.

"Well, I have my father's sister in Gary, Indiana. My mother has a cousin in Philadelphia, Pennsylvania. But I don't really know her that well," I say.

"Oh really. I've been to Philadelphia. Great city. Lots of American history there, although it's not like our history." He turns to his brother and they both laugh again.

"I don't know Indiana. Where are your parents? Are they making arrangements for the trip? I can give them some information if they would like," Roberto says.

"No, they're still in the South. I'm going to go over first and explore a little bit. I want to find a place to live and some job opportunities, and then they can come over. My aunt in Philadelphia might be able to help me when I get there," I say very confidently as if I have everything already planned out. I have no idea what I am talking about. I haven't even written my aunt in Philadelphia yet, and my mother hasn't spoken to her in years.

The men look at each other and half laugh.

"Signorina, it's a very difficult trip, not one a young girl should go on alone," he says in a condescending way.

"I mean, I know America is a very beautiful place, but it's not for everyone. But there is a lot of opportunity there, especially if you are a hard worker," he says.

"Oh, and I believe she is, at least that's what my wife says!" Signor Marino chimes in. He helps himself to a glass of water and pours one for his brother as well.

"Well, I'm sure. But still, a woman traveling alone to America? I would never let my daughter do that," Roberto says, and I start to dislike him.

My face is deceiving me, and I feel it getting red. I am a little embarrassed that I made such a confidant statement. But I really want to find out what to do, and how I can get to America.

"Well, what do you suggest I do then? I want to move my family to America. My aunt in Indiana started the paperwork, so it's just a matter of time before it's approved. What do I do next?" I ask curiously, really wanting to know from Roberto and Signor Marino what the process is that I need to follow.

Signor Marino explains. "A travel agency in town helps people make arrangements to go to America. You'll have to buy your tickets and go through the medical checks. You and your family will have to get physicals to make sure you're healthy. You have a lot to do, but start with the travel agency. They know the necessary steps to take."

Signora Marino finally joins us in the kitchen and greets her husband with a kiss.

"Roberto! So wonderful to see you again! I can't wait to hear all about your visit to America. And how was the trip? You look great!" Signora is rambling on in her usual breathless way as she goes to hug Roberto.

"I see you've met Claudia. She's a tremendous worker and has prepared a beautiful dinner for us. She made homemade orecchiette. Come on, go get cleaned up and we'll sit at the table." She directs the men where to go and they listen. She is definitely in charge right now.

The men do as they're told, and Signora Marino let's out a deep breath. "Thank you so much for all of your help today and for staying later. I'll see you tomorrow, first thing?" she asks.

"Certainly. Ciao Signora. I'll see you tomorrow morning," I assure her.

I am not sure how I feel about my exchange with the two men, but at least now I know where to start.

The next few weeks are much the same. I arrive every morning, start my chores, and end the day with food preparation. I am learning so much about cooking that it becomes my favorite part of the day. It's a nice environment, and I like working for Signora Marino, but I don't want to cook and clean for others forever.

Christmas is coming soon, and Signora Marino has a lot of extra work for me. She has many guests coming to stay overnight, and she's throwing lots of parties. She teaches me how to cook eel, which is a traditional holiday meal. I help her decorate the house with the Nativity scene and some beautiful greenery. Baby Jesus is in the middle of the manger, and his parents are looking hopefully at their child.

You can see the love in their expressions, and it makes me miss my mother and father.

I'm ironing sheets today. The clean white fabric lies smoothly on the board as I pass the hot iron over it. I can smell the heat coming from the fresh sheets, and my mind is wandering. Thinking of my home and how we don't have sheets like this. Thinking about how much I've already changed in my life with just this move to the North.

I wonder what Paola is doing and if she has any stories she wants to tell me. I definitely have a lot I want to tell her. I find myself wishing I could talk to her, but I resolve in my mind that I'll write her a letter when I get home.

"Claudia, what are you daydreaming about?" Signora Marino asks me.

"Oh, I'm just thinking about my family. I miss them, especially around the holidays. But it's too expensive for either of us to travel, so we can only write letters," I say sadly.

"I understand. I'm sure it's lonely for you to be here all by yourself. I can't imagine how you got here." She shakes her head in disbelief. "But you have your aunt and uncle, right?" she asks.

"Yes, they are wonderful," I say, but deep down inside I know that they don't really take the place of my family. I miss them, but I know I will see them again someday.

I finish my workday and begin walking home. In my mind, I go back to Mary and Joseph and how they were traveling when Jesus was born. How difficult of a trip it was and how they weren't welcomed. I think of my family and how I want them to come to America, too. Will we be welcomed there?

I realize I need to be on that boat someday soon.

I think about what I need to do to accomplish this goal, and of course money comes to mind. I'm saving all the money I'm making with my cleaning job, but I don't have any idea how much it will cost to go to America on the boat.

I decide this weekend I will go visit the travel agency that Signor Marino mentioned. I ask Zia Nadia about it when I get home.

"Zia, what do you know about going to America?" I ask cautiously, a little apprehensive to bring it up, but I do, anyway.

"Well, I know you can go by boat. Some people go by plane, but that's for the very rich. It's expensive either way." Zia Nadia's eyes raise and her forehead wrinkles.

Flying in an airplane seems like a dream to me. I have seen it on television before, advertisements for it. *Alitalia Airline, they can take you anywhere you want to go.* It would be a lot faster than a boat ride to America. It seems so luxurious, and I'm pretty sure I can't afford that.

Zia Nadia continues. "It's a long trip on the water, about a week or so, I've heard. And sometimes it can be rough. I don't know how much it costs since I never thought about it. Why are you asking?" She questions me.

"Well, Signora Marino's husband has a brother who came to visit a few weeks ago. He came from America by boat to Genoa, and they picked him up there. It just made me think that I could get a ticket and go to America someday. Signor Marino works for the United States Consulate, and he told me what the process is. I have two aunts in America, and you know one is in Philadelphia, Zia Nina. Maybe I can go visit her?" I say.

"Ma devi essere pazza! You must be crazy! You can't go to America by yourself. How would you do that?" she says, suggesting that I'm crazy to even think it.

"Zia, why can't I go by myself? I came here by myself. It's just a little farther away." I'm trying to sound confident, but I'm fooling myself a little. I know it will be scary, but I really want to go. "Besides, like I said, I have some family there," I remind her.

She shakes her head and says, "Claudia, you want too much. That's your problem. You're never satisfied with what you have. You should be happy with the life you have here. It's a good life. You have a job, and you can get an apartment soon. I'm sure you'll find a man and make a nice life together. Why would you want to go to America? The men there are no good. They don't take care of their families the way Italian men do," she says convincingly.

I laugh a little inside. That's not my experience with Italian men. But that's not what I'm interested in, anyway. I want to go to America. I want to learn to speak English, and I want an education. I know this for sure, and I'm not changing my mind.

"Zia, I'm going to do this. If you want to help me, great, if not I'm sure I can figure it out on my own." I feel bad for speaking to my aunt like this, since she's been so good to me, but the more we talk, the more serious I become.

"I'm going to write a letter to your mother. How do you think she will feel if she knows you are planning to go to America now by yourself? You're going to make her sick!" As my aunt says this, I remember a time when I was young.

The last time she was sick with worry she had a stroke. I remember it like it was yesterday. It was when my little brother Franco fell and got hurt. The front door to our house broke off the hinges from a strong wind and landed on top of him. She thought he was dead for sure. He was fine, but the next morning she woke up and half of her face was paralyzed. We knew it was from the big shock the day before.

Now my aunt is yelling at me, and I can see her anger is growing.

"Zia, please, I'm not trying to make you mad. I'm not even sure why you're getting mad?" I ask.

"Because it's not safe! You can't go alone. Girls don't travel alone like that to another country! It's a stupid idea…un'idea stupida!" she says again.

"It's not a stupid idea!" I'm yelling now. "I have a dream of living in America someday, and I know I have to follow it. Why do you think it's stupid? So many people leave Italy and go to America. There are more jobs and better opportunities in education. The living conditions are better, too. I know you've done a lot for me, and I appreciate everything, but I am going to do this!" I say, asserting my position.

I can feel that my face is red, and I have my hands on my hips. I'm angry now, too, and I'm not backing down. She starts to calm a little bit, and we speak more quietly to each other.

"Gioia, I'm worried about you doing this. I don't know how to help you with this crazy dream." She shakes her head and walks toward the kitchen to get a little glass of wine. She pours me one, too, and we sit at the table together.

"Zia, don't worry. I went from Orsara to Foggia to Chieri, all on my own. I can figure this out, too." I'm not sure why I think it's the same thing, but I'm trying to convince her, and maybe myself, that it is.

"I don't know where you get your strength, but I wish I had some of it." She holds her glass up and we salute each other.

"To wanting more and having the strength to fight for it!" I say as our glasses clink together.

CHAPTER 18

———

The sun is barely up, and the room feels cold this morning. As soon as I wake up, I think about my mother and that I need to write her and let her know my plan. I don't want to worry her, so I think if she hears it from me directly, she'll be okay. Before anything else, I get a pad of paper and pencil from the dresser and sit on my bed to write.

I'm careful to word my letter in a way that will show my mother I'm capable. I write out my plan and let her know how I will eventually move the whole family over. Seeing it there in ink makes it feel real to me, and I'm excited to send it off.

My aunt and uncle are still asleep, so I get myself ready quietly without disturbing them. I need to go to the travel office, too, so I prepare my purse with a little money and the letter and sneak out of the house.

It's December, and the morning air is crisp. I exhale into the beauty of the day with a cloud of smoke that disappears as soon as it arrives. Even though the sun is shining, I can't seem to forget the cold.

In my excitement, I didn't realize that it's a little too early and the post office and travel agency don't open for another hour, so I find a bar and sit to have an espresso. I like the time alone. Between working for the Marinos and living with my aunt and uncle, I don't get much alone time.

I enjoy the peaceful quiet of the bar for a little and then leave to walk around town, killing time. I go to the post office first and drop the letter. Then I make my way to the travel agency, and when I arrive, I'm greeted by posters everywhere. Exotic places to visit shown in brilliant color all over the walls. Posters of luxurious cruise liners with extremely well-dressed people on board.

I'm nervous, and very excited at the same time.

"Ciao Signore. I'd like information on how to travel to America," I say. I want to appear confident that I can go.

He looks above his glasses without moving his head. "Do you have your clearances?"

"I'm working on that, but I would like to know when the boat leaves from Genoa, and how much it costs, please?" I ask. I have some money that I've been saving already in my purse.

"Si, okay. Well, a boat leaves every couple of weeks or so. The *Cristoforo Colombo* and the *Leonardo da Vinci*. Both are very beautiful boats, not very old, and they're nicely appointed. They sail on a rotating schedule. When do you want to travel, and how many travelers are there?" He flips pages in a ledger style book as he talks.

I heard about the *Leonardo da Vinci*. It's newer than the *Cristoforo Colombo* and was built to replace the *Andrea Doria* that struck a Swedish boat and sank. It was on its way into New York when it happened. It was a big news story. But I don't know anything about the *Cristoforo Colombo*. And frankly I really don't care which boat I'm on.

"Well how much is it for one ticket? Nothing fancy, the least expensive option there is please," I say.

He looks at me over his glasses again and asks, "Who is this ticket for?"

"For me, sir," I say honestly.

With a puzzled expression he asks, "How old are you?"

"I'm eighteen and old enough to travel on my own," I say, annoyed that he's questioning me.

"Si, yes, I understand." He quickly realizes his questions are offensive. He changes his approach and offers me the information I asked for. "If you travel in Tourist Class, they have space leaving next week, and the fare is 155,000 lire."

My knees buckle. I don't have that much money with me or even saved for that matter.

"How long is the trip?" I ask hesitantly, wondering how I'm going to make this work.

"It's eight days. It's a beautiful luxury liner, Italy's finest!" He's boasting about the beauty of the boat while I worry about how I'm going to pay for it. He sees in my expression that I'm grappling with this dilemma and offers up a good suggestion.

"Signorina, most people don't pay at once. They set up a payment plan. You can come and pay a little at a time while you work on your clearances. Then when you're ready, we'll pick a date for you to travel. How does that sound?" he says reasonably.

Oh, what a relief!

"Oh mille grazie, Signore!" I am so happy to know that I can pay a little at a time. I'm still waiting to hear if we are approved to travel so this works out perfectly. I pay him the first installment that I have available with me in my purse, take my receipt, and leave. But not before telling him that I would be back every week to pay a little toward my ticket.

My feet hardly touch the ground as I walk out of the agency.

I just made my first payment to travel to America!

I figure it will take several months to pay for the ticket and also save enough to travel with, but I am so determined now. Nothing is going to stop me. I can figure out all the details when I get home.

———

I get home in time for lunch with Zia Nadia and Zio Marco. With a big smile on my face, I sit at the kitchen table beaming with excitement.

"Oh, Claudia, what have you been up to? You look like you're in love, so happy with rosy cheeks!" My aunt giggles a little in embarrassment for me; my uncle rolls his eyes at her.

"No Zia, I went to pay some money toward my ticket to America. It's 155,000 lire, and I made the first payment today." I'm still on a high from the morning when she reminds me about my mother.

"Gioia, you must write your mother and make sure…"

"Ah Zia, I already did. I sent my mother a letter this morning on my way to the agency. She's going to know exactly what my plan is within a few days. Besides, it'll take some time for me to pay for the ticket and save enough money for the trip, so I'm not leaving just yet," I say, reassuring her that I've thought of everything.

Zia Nadia claps her hands in appreciation.

"Grazie Dio! Maybe I can change your mind!" She looks at me, wondering.

But she knows as well as I do that's not happening. I smile as if to say "good luck," and she understands right away. I think she knows it's a losing battle with me now, so she's not going to fight it.

"Do you have Zia Nina's address in Philadelphia? I'd like to write her and see if I can go to her house when I get there. Do you think she'll let me?" I ask Zia Nadia.

"Si, Zia Nina, will definitely help you. She would be offended if you went to America and didn't make arrangements to see her. I'll find the address, and we can write her together after we eat," my aunt says.

"That's great! Come on, Zia, let's have lunch. I have a lot to figure out before my trip. Actually, I need to find out what's happening with the application approval. We can write Zia Lucia, too. She'll know what's going on." We enjoy a beautiful lunch, and then I go to my room to do some calculations.

I need to plan for the cost of the ticket, money needed for eight days' worth of food on the boat, money needed for a taxi when I get to New York, some new clothes to travel with, and maybe a new suitcase. That's a little splurge, but I can't travel with the one I have—it's worn down to nothing and dirty.

I'm not really sure how much I need for taxis in New York. But I know how much taxis are here, so I add a little extra just in case. It's definitely going to take a long time to get this together. But that's okay, I need to wait for my clearance from Zia Lucia and then get a physical.

I think my plan may actually work!

I sit on my bed and write a letter to Zia Lucia to ask about the application.
I really hope she can give me some good news.

Two weeks and we are into the New Year. I get a letter back from Zia Lucia saying she doesn't know what the status of the application is. She submitted everything a couple of years ago as soon as she got back home to America from her visit with us. She says my mother should have received a letter or I could check with the Consulate.

I still haven't heard back from my mother, so I decide we better call her. I need an answer quickly and can't wait to send her a letter. Again, we go to the post office so they can call the one in Orsara.

The man in the post office makes the call and hands me the phone.

It rings a few times, and I hear a voice answer.

"Pronto," says the man on the phone.

"Pronto, I'm calling to send a message to my mother, Josefina Valentino. She lives at 31 Via Silvio Pellico. My name is Claudia Valentino." I give him as much information up front as I think he probably needs.

"Si Signorina. I know your mother. What's your message?"

I know I don't have much time, so I speak fast.

"Please tell her I need to know if she received the letter from the United States Consulate approving our application to go to America. She can send me a letter with the details," I explain to the man in Orsara.

"What are you saying Signorina? I don't understand." He says. The line was gritty and it sounded like he was a million miles away.

"Please tell her I need to know if she received anything from the Consulate…" I'm screaming now, but slowly.

"Sir, please tell her to send me a letter and let me know if she heard from the United States Consulate." I continue to scream.

"She knows where to find me. The letter from the Consulate. Ask her to mail it to me. It's her daughter, Claudia...." I scream again.

And the line goes dead with a long, deep continuous buzz.

Well at least I got my message to him and hopefully my mother will mail me a letter soon.

I go back to work more excited than usual. My employer notices how happy I am and asks me why. I probably shouldn't tell her, but I'm too excited to contain myself.

"I'm planning to go to America. Our family's application was submitted a long time ago, and I'm waiting to get the approval. Now we just have to save enough money to travel. I'm going to go first and send for my family later," I explain.

Signora Marino drops her shoulders into a disappointed slump. "Oh, Claudia, you can't leave me. What will I do without you?"

"It'll be a while before I can go; I have to save a lot of money. I promise I'll make sure you're okay before I leave." I say sincerely. "I have been wanting to go for several years now, and I'm ready."

Knowing she isn't happy with this, I continue, "But like I said, I have to save money, so it'll be a few months at least. I also have to get a physical with the doctor and go through my medical clearances. I can still work for you, and maybe we can find my replacement and I can train her?" I say hoping she doesn't get upset.

Signora Marino seems happy with that solution. "Well, I can't imagine anyone will be as good as you, but maybe with your training she'll be okay. Come on, let's get back to work. We're making pasta with beans tonight. Signor Marino loves that."

———————

It's the end of January and a letter is delivered to Zia Nadia's house from my mother. I am so excited to open it that I can hardly wait. I sit at the kitchen table, feverishly tearing the envelope and pulling out the papers; a letter written from my mother and the letter from the Consulate.

Dear Claudia,

I was happy to get your message. I got these papers a long time ago, but I didn't know what you wanted me to do with them. When did you decide to go to America? I wish our whole family could go, but right now you know it's impossible. Here is the information so you can do what you need.

Everyone here is okay. Paola has a good job. She's saving money and wants to move to Switzerland. A hospital in Zurich needs help in the kitchen and laundry. A few girls from town are going, and Paola wants to go, too. I think she learned it from you.

Oh, how happy it makes me to hear what my sister Paola is doing! My mother goes on to talk about the younger kids. They're all still in school and learning how to take care of themselves pretty well. Everyone seems okay, and I feel relieved.

Let us know when you're planning to travel. My cousin Nina is in Philadelphia and I know she will help you. I will write her a letter, but you should write her too. Then you can give her all the details.

Our application has been approved, and all of us could go to America!

It's finally happening!

I can hardly contain my excitement as I jump out of my seat and dance around right there in the kitchen!

I read through the rest of the letter as well as the approved application to travel. It says we have two years to move everyone over. I must go to the Consulate to show them my papers and get a physical. I have to get the medical clearance before they will let me take the trip. That should be easy. I can't remember the last time I was sick.

Then my mother wishes me a happy New Year.

I wonder how they spent the holiday.

I miss them all so much, but the happiness I feel right now makes me forget the pain of longing for all of my family to be together again someday.

CHAPTER 19

———

When the weekend comes, I make my usual trip to the agency to make my weekly payment for my ticket.

"Ciao Signore. How are you today?" I ask the man behind the desk. He's smiling and in a pleasant mood.

"Oh Signorina, I'm good. How are you? It's nice to see you again," he says happily.

"I'm fine, thank you. Can you tell me how much more I owe after this payment?" I've been paying for a couple of months, and I know I still have a lot to go, but I'm making a lot of progress on it. I should be able to plan my travel soon.

"Oh Signora, you still have about 110,000 lire to pay, but you're doing well. Just keep coming in and paying a little each week. Before you know it, you'll be ready to travel." He says confidently. I'm sure he sees this all the time.

"Thank you," I say, a little disappointed. I knew I still had a lot to pay, but I guess the amount hit hard. It feels a little overwhelming, like it'll take forever to get there. I try not to worry about it and head to the Consulate to get any information I can from them.

When I arrive at the Consulate office, a long line of people are waiting to get in. I take out my booklet and pencil and go over my calculations. I think it'll take me about five or six more months to save enough money. That will bring me to the summer, and I think traveling in the summer on a boat would be ideal.

Right now, the weather is cold and there's a feeling of rain in the air. There's a new season struggling to be born, though; I can feel it as I stand in line. I wait for almost an hour before I get in.

When I finally enter the building, I'm shocked by its beauty. The floors are white and black marble, the columns are tall, and the ceilings are high and domed. It's a very old building, and I sense the history all around me. When it's my turn, I walk up to the woman behind the desk.

"Ciao. I want to travel to America, and I need to know how much time I need to get my medical clearance and paperwork?" I ask politely.

"Well Signorina, do you have the letter from the Consulate giving you permission to travel?" The woman behind the desk asks.

"Yes, I have it here," I say as I hand her the letter. She looks it over quickly and sees that I'm cleared to travel.

"Okay then, we just need to schedule your medical visit. I can do that with you right now." She says happily and pulls out her scheduling book.

"It looks like I can give you an appointment in about a month." She goes over the dates that are available, and we pick one on a weekend so I don't have to take any days off from Signora Marino's house.

I fill out the paperwork and thank her for her help.

I tell her I'll be back in a month.

Each week I continue to make my payments for the travel agency. I get closer and closer to my goal, and everything seems to be falling into place.

The day of my medical appointment with the Consulate comes, and I make sure to be there early. As soon as I arrive, I see a long line again, but since I have an appointment, I don't have to wait. They check me in and bring me back to the area where the medical staff is.

A nurse pokes a needle in my arm and gets a couple vials of blood. I wait for the doctor, and when he comes in and examines me, he assures me that everything is fine. Once they have the blood results, they can give me the certificate I need. They say to come back next week.

The next week I promptly arrive at the Consulate, the first one in the medical line. I ask to see my results and get my certificate.

"I'm sorry Signorina, mi dispiace, but your blood results are not good." My heart drops into my stomach.

"Wh...Wh....What do you mean not good?" I feel my face turning red again. I don't understand what they are saying to me right now.

"I'm sorry, but you have the bacteria for tuberculosis. Do you know what that is?" the nurse asks gingerly.

"No, I have no idea what that is." I'm getting upset.

I can't stop the flood of tears.

I'm trying to hold it together, but it's not working.

"Signorina, please don't cry. We don't know what this means yet. We'll have to do a chest X-ray and then we can tell if it's a problem or not. Okay? Please don't cry." She goes on explaining what the disease is and what happens if you have it.

I am hardly paying attention at this point.

All I hear is I can't go to America.

She calms me down a little, but now I'm so scared. What if I'm not allowed to travel? That thought has never occurred to me—that my health would be a problem! I never get sick. And I feel totally fine.

I can't believe this is happening.

The nurse says they don't have anyone to do the X-ray on Saturday, so I'll have to come during the week. I make the first available appointment for Thursday afternoon, two weeks from now. I will just have to leave work early that day. I'm sure Signora Marino won't mind. I've already started training a new girl, and she's doing very well.

All I want to do is move to America. I never in a million years thought I could be denied for health reasons. Why would that even happen? And how did I get this ridiculous bacteria I never heard of?

I was going to stop at the agency to make a payment toward my ticket, but I'm not going to bother doing that now. I just want to get home and be alone in my room.

When I walk in, Zia Nadia and Zio Marco are in the kitchen, fighting over what to have for lunch. Their voices are loud but as soon as they see me, they quiet down. They can tell something's wrong.

"Claudia, what happened?" Zia Nadia asks as I fall in a chair and begin to cry again.

"They said I have some kind of bacteria, and I might not be allowed to travel to America. I can't believe this is happening to me, Zia." My sadness is unbearable. My hands are shaking, and I feel my whole body ache.

"Oh Dio, what did they say? Are you sick?" She looks confused.

Zio Marco asks, "What do you mean, bacteria? What bacteria?"

"I don't know. They say it's tuberculosis. And no, Zia, that's what makes me so mad. I feel totally fine. I'm not sick at all!" I'm getting worked up again just talking about it.

My aunt and uncle know what tuberculosis is. They say they've known some people who had it in the past, but they didn't know that much about it.

"So, what did they tell you to do?" Zia Nadia rubs my arm and I feel my shoulders relax.

"I just have to go back in a couple of weeks to get an X-ray. I guess then they'll know if I'm okay to travel or not. Zia, what am I going to do if they stop me from traveling?" I let out a deep breath, as I let it all sink in.

"Gioia, don't worry. Let's see what the X-rays say, and if you can't travel to America, we'll figure it out. Maybe you can take some medicine to cure it? We'll take you to our doctor if we need to." She tries very hard to make me feel better, but it's not working.

"Grazie, Zia. I think I'm going to go lie down." I get up, and she touches my hand.

"Don't you want to eat first, then go lie down? Sit here with us while I make lunch."

"No Zia, I'm not hungry, anyway. I'm just going to lie down for a little. Grazie." My head and shoulders drop down as I leave the kitchen. I get to my room, close the door, and fall on the bed. I cry into the pillow and fall asleep.

I wake up to rain drops hitting the roof loudly and the realization that this setback is real and not a dream. I don't know how long I slept, but I feel better. I actually think I slept through the disappointment.

There's nothing I can do.

I just have to wait for the X-ray and go from there.

I can't worry about it beyond that.

The next two weeks are the longest of my life, and when the day finally comes, I get up feeling very nervous.

My hands are shaking, and my stomach feels nauseous.

I go to work in the morning but leave just after lunch for my appointment.

I take a taxi to the Consulate since I don't have the motivation to walk there today. I'm feeling so anxious, and I just want to get there quickly. When I arrive, they take me back, and the nurse prepares me for the X-ray. She explains the process to me, but I tell her I already know it. I had an X-ray of my hand in the hospital in Foggia.

They x-ray me and tell me to get my things and go wait in the waiting room. A doctor will look at it and they will let me know the results.

My nerves are getting the best of me, and I drop my purse as I'm gathering my things.

Everything splatters out all over the floor, and I scramble to pick it all up.

My hands are still shaking, and my eyes are welling.

The wait is excruciating.

I sit by myself thinking about the two possible outcomes. If they tell me I can't go, maybe it wasn't meant to be. Maybe this has just been a crazy dream and I should give it up. But if they tell me I can go, then my whole world will be changed forever. I'm sick with anticipation of the result.

About an hour goes by, and finally the nurse walks out with a paper in her hand. "Good news, Claudia. You are okay to travel. You only have the bacteria, not active tuberculosis, so I guess I should say congratulations!" The nurse hands me the paper and tries to walk away. I jump up from my chair and hug her tightly. I think she's taken by surprise.

"Oh, thank you so much!" I say, clutching the paper. Suddenly I feel alive again!

This news just instantly ripped me out of the fog I've been in over the last couple of weeks.

I can go to America!

I'm still squeezing the nurse so hard that she tries to push away from me.

"Okay Signorina, here's your paperwork. This clearance is good for two months, so please make your arrangements quickly. I don't want you to have any other delays!" I take her advice with appreciation.

I don't want any other delays, either, and I plan to travel before the time is up, anyway.

No matter what it takes.

On my way home, I stop at the travel agency again to check on my ticket. I want to make another payment and schedule my trip.

"Ciao Signore!" I say, excited to show him that I've been cleared to travel. "How many more payments do I need to make to get my ticket?"

"Wonderful Signora. This is great news. You only need to make a few more payments, so let's pick the travel day now." He picks up his ledger and flips through the pages.

"Sette Luglio on the Cristoforo Colombo. How's that? Okay?" He asks.

"Si, perfecto. I have only two months before my clearances expire so that's perfect. Thank you, Signore." I leave feeling happy. It's finally scheduled.

I'm leaving for America on July seventh!

On my way home, I stop in a consignment shop in town near the travel agency. I want to get a suitcase, and I can't afford much. They have some nice options in the store that are inexpensive, and I choose one, pay a deposit, and ask the owner to hold it for me until I can come back with the rest of the money. On my way out of the store, I see a beautiful pink suit on a mannequin in the corner. It has a few small signs of wear, but otherwise it's striking, and I think it's just my size.

Wouldn't that be beautiful to travel in?

I try it on, and it fits like a glove.

The store clerk smiles and holds it for me as well, and I walk out happy.

When I arrive back home, Zia Nadia is waiting for me in the kitchen.

"Gioia, is that you?" my aunt asks.

I run into the kitchen, drop my things, and hug her screaming, "Everything is okay! I can travel, Zia! I'm leaving on the Cristoforo Colombo on July seventh."

"Oh Grazie Dio! I was so worried. Oh, thank God!" My aunt says as she hugs me tighter, and I feel good in her arms. It feels familiar and warm.

I tell her about my new suitcase and pink suit, and then I go to my room to think things through. I have a lot to figure out. Next week, I'll pick up my things at the consignment shop and a few other items I'll need for the trip. The travel agency tells me the boat has a swimming pool and restaurants. I need a bathing suit, too. A red one.

All this planning is making me hopeful.

This is really happening!

I pull out my pad of paper to make a list and write a schedule for when I will pick everything up. I still have to work every day right up until the end, so I will only have the weekends to get ready. I can make a couple stops after work, too, but only for small, easy purchases.

I also write a letter to my mother. I have to let her and Paola know that my travel date is set.

The next few weeks go as planned, and I manage to purchase some personal toiletries, a pair of cropped pants with two blouses to match, a bathing suit, and a pair of flat shoes. I thought they might be more comfortable for walking around on the boat. Approximately eleven hundred people are going on this trip; I can't imagine how big this boat is going to be.

Time flies by, and my day of travel has finally arrived. It's the seventh of July and I wake up before the sun. I find that I am so excited that I can hardly sleep.

Zia Nadia and Zio Marco are going to take me to Genoa to see me off.

I'm up, dressed, and packed, waiting in the kitchen when Zia Nadia comes in. It's barely light out, but I'm ready.

"Oh Gioia, you scared me! I wasn't expecting you to be sitting here already! The day is finally here!" She acts excited for me, but I know she's worried.

I'm only eighteen, and I'm traveling alone.

"Buon giorno, Zia! I could hardly sleep through the night. We have to leave soon; I don't want to miss the boat," I say as if she doesn't already know this.

"I know, Gioia. We're fine. It's only about two hours to Genoa. We have time. I'll go wake Marco and we'll get on the road soon." She gets the espresso pot ready and puts it on the stove before she goes to wake my uncle.

I am feeling nostalgic, so I close my eyes and take it all in. The sound of my aunt shuffling through the kitchen in her slippers, the smell of the espresso on the stove, the warmth of their home, and the feeling that everything is about to change all hit me like a ton of bricks.

The ride to Genoa feels like it's taking eight hours instead of two. We pull into Genoa in a car my uncle borrowed from his friend, and I see the traffic heading toward the docks. Cars everywhere waiting in line to bring passengers to their adventures.

I realize that I'm not the only person excited to get on with this trip.

My uncle parks the car, and he gets my suitcase out. He carries it for me up to the area where the luggage needs to go. And I see it.

There it is!

The *Cristoforo Colombo!*

Written in big black lettering along the front of the boat.

It has a strong presence, like nothing I've ever seen before. It's an enormous ship with a black body and white along the top; flags waving majestically high up into the air. I am enamored with her beauty.

What a marvel!

I check my luggage and continue toward the gangway to go on board. I feel a lump in my throat. Am I really doing this? What kind of girl travels alone like this to a foreign country?

Suddenly I feel a little queasy.

I'm dressed in my confident pink suit and a lovely string of pearls my aunt gave me as a parting gift. I don't know if they are real, but they mean something to her so I'm proud to wear them.

Everyone entering the boat is excited. Talking, laughing, and hugging. I am amazed at the happiness this vessel is bringing to all onboard. It's like a party; a mix of people who are taking the trip and those who are sending them off. Everyone is dressed in their best outfits, women in colorful suits with white gloves, men in suits and ties. It's breathtaking!

"Oh, can you believe it? I'm actually here!" I exclaim to my aunt and uncle. They are just trying to shuffle me forward through the crowd as my head is turning left to right trying to take it all in. Green velvet fabric on the sofas, beautiful clocks on the mantels, it is a sight!

We get to a point where it's time to say goodbye, so I pose for a quick picture that my uncle takes before they leave. I tell them I'll go to the front of the boat and wave to them from there. They each give me a long hug and I feel their concern, their sadness, but also their excitement for me. I'm so happy to be going to America, but sad to be leaving Italy.

"Oh, thank you so much for everything!" I hug both my aunt and uncle at the same time, my arms around their necks not wanting to let go. "I could not have gotten here without your help."

"Good luck, Gioia, and be careful! And make sure you write as soon as you arrive." My aunt gives me one last kiss.

They leave, and I rush up to an open spot in the front of the boat. I'm ready to wave goodbye as I spot their small figures down on the dock. Goodbye to everything I've known my whole life.

The tugboats are already hooked up and ready. The stacks are blowing smoke in the air and the horns are sounding. I raise my arm to wave, and I begin to cry a little. I'm so scared, but so excited all at once. These competing feelings are overwhelming me as I wave to them feverishly.

The boat begins to move.
What awaits me in America?
There's no turning back now.
I'm on my way, and only God knows what I'll find when
I get there!

CHAPTER 20

———

Being alone for the first time in my life is both frightening and exciting. I wave away my aunt and uncle and my whole life in Italy and turn completely toward the next eight days on this boat.

Eight days before I will reach America and see things in person that I have only seen on television or in newspapers. It's a glorious thought!

The boat slowly leaves the dock, and everyone is waving and happy. The sun is shining, and the air has the fresh smell of the sea. The party that is occurring on deck is like nothing I have ever experienced. People are hugging anyone standing next to them, even strangers.

I am in awe of the entire scene.

"Hey what's your name?" I hear a voice from just behind me. I turn to find a very handsome, blond, blue-eyed man. He's speaking very fast, and I have trouble keeping up.

"Wait, aspetta." I hold my hand up to stop him from talking. "I don't speak English very well." I ask him to slow down.

"Oh, I'm sorry," he says. "My name is David Moore. Are you excited for our trip? I know we have a couple of stops

before we cross the Atlantic, but I can't wait to get back home."
He's trying very hard to speak slowly in Italian, acting out his
words in a very dramatic way. I giggle at his theatrics, and
I'm very impressed at how well he speaks.

"Oh, am I funny?" He's giggling, too now, and we both
start laughing. We turn to watch the rest of the departure
from the dock. It was getting smaller and smaller and many
of the people were already starting to leave.

"So, you didn't tell me your name." He gives me a smirk
and waits for me to answer.

"Claudia Valentino." I reach my gloved hand out to
greet him.

"Hmm that sounds pretty much like an Italian name. I
guess this trip isn't taking you home?"

"Oh yes, it is, David!" I say with confidence.

"Well then, let's go celebrate!" David starts to lead the
way down the steps to the nearest bar. The bartenders are
pouring glasses of orange juice and champagne and have
them lined up on the bar for anyone to take. David grabs
two and hands me one.

"Here have a mimosa." He lifts his glass. "Cheers! Or
maybe I should say salute?" He smiles proudly.

I lift my glass and tap his. "Salute!" I take a sip and it
tastes delicious. It's the first time I've ever had such a drink.

"What did you call this drink?" I ask as I take another sip.

"It's a mimosa. It's a nice drink for the morning." He
downs his in one last gulp and grabs another.

"So, David, where are you from?" I am curious about
where my new friend lives in America.

"I live in Ithaca, New York. I just graduated from college
a few months ago, and my parents gave me this trip to Italy."
I'm mesmerized by his eyes so blue. Like the sea.

"Well, that's a nice gift they gave you." I can't imagine such a gift. He must come from a wealthy family. "I never heard of that town. Is it near New York City?"

"Not really, it's about a four-hour drive from the city. My parents are coming to meet me when we arrive." The boat was beginning to move faster, and the party was still going strong. I wanted to get to my room and get settled in.

"David, thank you and it was very nice to speak to you, but I'd like to unpack." I take the last sip of my drink and set the empty glass down on the bar. My head is feeling a little foggy, but in a good way.

"Of course. I'm going to head to my room, too. Maybe we can meet again another time, possibly tonight for dinner?" His head turns to the side as he waits for my response.

I feel a little overwhelmed by my day already, and it's still morning. "No, David, I think tonight I'm going to take it easy. First time on a boat and all."

"Okay, maybe tomorrow. I'm sure I'll see you around the boat." He smiles and escorts me to the elevators. He kindly waits until the car comes and I get on. I push the button to go down to my level and the doors close slowly, David disappearing behind them.

I take a deep breath and let it out. I think about what David said and how he was traveling as a gift. I imagine a whole world of people who travel this way. Oh, how behind the times my little town seems now.

In my stateroom, my suitcase is already there waiting for me. The room is very small, with two beds, green floor tiles, a wooden dresser, and one chair with mauve velvet upholstery. It doesn't look like anyone else is staying in this room with me, so I take the bottom bunk and begin to unpack my bag. I put my toiletries away in a small, attached room with a toilet and sink.

The ship is really moving now, and I can feel the gentle sway of it. My stomach feels a little queasy and I'm sure it's from the excitement, or maybe the mimosa. I put my case away in a compartment under my bed and lie down.

When I wake up, I feel very sick to my stomach. My mouth is watering, and I think I'm going to throw up. I lift my head from the pillow and feel the urgency, so I frantically get up and put my face over the toilet and let it all go.

Oh God, this feeling is awful. I throw up for what feels like a half hour, and then I rinse my face and go back to bed. I have never felt so terrible in my whole life. The room feels like it's spinning, and my stomach still feels queasy after all that.

I fall somewhere in between sleep and being awake and I start dreaming. I see my family all together in our little house in Orsara. My sister Paola is fixing the table for dinner, and I'm helping our mother with the pasta. Our table is much larger in my dream, with a pretty blue and yellow tablecloth and white dishes. Mama is at the sink washing the greens for dinner. All my other brothers and sisters are running around laughing and playing. Everyone is dressed up and clean.

I am ripped out of my dream with that queasy feeling again, so I quickly jump up and run to the toilet.

The rest of the day goes like this, lying in bed, throwing up. The boat is rocking around, and with each sway side to side I feel sicker and sicker. I try to sleep so I don't feel the fear of having to go through this for eight days. I fall asleep with nothing left in my stomach and no energy to dream.

The next morning, I feel somewhat better when I wake up. The boat seems calmer, so I wash up, put on my new cropped pants with a plain cotton shirt and flat shoes, and decide maybe some fresh air would be a good idea.

I make my way to one of the pools. The sun is shining and it's a very warm day. I should have put my new bathing suit on, but my stomach is still too uneasy. The pool is full of people tossing around big, striped beach balls and splashing each other. I find a deck chair and lie down. The air feels nice, and the sounds on deck make me happy.

Crewmen in white uniforms and round hats are working around the pool. One stops to ask me if I am okay.

"I think I'm a little seasick. I don't feel very good, and I haven't eaten anything." I say quietly, trying not to lose it right there on the pool deck.

"Well, miss, then you should eat a little bread and maybe have some bubbly water. It'll make your stomach feel better. Can I bring you some?" he asks politely.

"Oh, I'm sorry I didn't bring any money to the pool with me," I say, embarrassed that I wouldn't have thought to do that.

"No problem, miss, everything on the boat is complimentary. All your meals are included, so I will bring you a little something that will help your stomach. And if it's still bad, you can see the ship's infirmary. They can give you something that'll help. I'll be right back." He turns to walk away.

Oh, bread and bubbly water sounds perfect. And how did I not know that I didn't have to pay for the food? I guess I never asked the travel agent back in Chieri.

The kind crewman returned with a tray and handed me a little plate with bread and a glass of bubbly water. I was a little afraid to eat it, but I was so hungry that I couldn't hold back. I ate it slowly and took small sips, and my stomach seemed to be okay.

"Well hello, Claudia. I thought I'd see you last night. How's everything going so far?" David was standing over me.

"Oh, David I was very sick all night. I think the sea doesn't agree with my stomach. Did you feel ill at all? It was so rough." I was hoping not to be alone in this misery.

"Well, it was a little rocky at first but it didn't bother me. It's pretty calm now, though. Are you feeling okay?" He sits on my lounge chair next to me and puts a hand on my leg.

I sit up, a little startled by his touch. "I'm feeling a little better, but I just ate bread so we'll see how that goes." I say as he removes his hand from my leg.

"Well maybe you'll be okay in time for dinner. Do you want to try it? Seas are calm now, so it should be a good night," he asks politely.

"I really don't know how I'm going to feel, but if I feel good, I'd be happy to join you for dinner. What time shall I meet you there?" I say, hoping I feel okay. I really would like to have a nice dinner, and I don't want to go alone. The bread I just ate certainly wasn't satisfying.

"Great. Meet me at six o'clock in the First-Class Dining Room!" He gets up to leave. "I hope to see you tonight!"

"Wait. I'm not staying in first class." I say, unsure of how this works.

"That's no problem. You're my guest!" He flashes an adorable smile, puts his hands in his pockets, and walks away.

First class for dinner! This will definitely be a new experience for me. I put my head back down on the lounge chair and close my eyes. The sun and fresh air feel good, and I think my sickness may have passed. I relax in the sun with the sounds of life all around me.

The splashing, the laughs, the music in the background. It's all beautiful to me. I stayed there for a couple of hours just watching the fun from my chair, but then I felt like exploring the ship a bit.

The ship has several small gift shops that offer items passengers may have forgotten, in addition to post cards and chocolates. I stop in just to look around. The lounges have dark walls, beautiful circular sofas, and red velvet chairs. Everything looks so rich and fancy; it is a very different lifestyle than I am used to.

Ship employees are everywhere, always asking if I need anything. Everyone speaks both Italian and English very well, and I am envious. I want to learn to speak English perfectly, too. Aside from the seasickness, I really like being on this ship.

I get back to my room in time for a short rest and some time to write a few letters. I write my parents, Zia Anna, and Zia Nadia and let them know how great the boat is. I describe every inch of what I've seen so far in great detail. I tell them the trip is eight days long and by the time they read this, I'll be in America. I prepare the letters so I can put them in the mail slot on my way to dinner.

I feel good, so I put on the light green dress that Signor Sarto made for me and my black heels. I tie my hair up in a bun and try to look as fancy as possible for my dinner with David.

On my way, I drop the letters in the mail and walk into the First-Class Dining Room, feeling a little intimidated. David is waiting for me by the bar, so I walk quickly over to him. He's dashing in a beautiful pale-gray suit, made in a lightweight fabric. It looks like it was specially tailored for him.

"Wow, you look beautiful in that dress, and I'm glad you're feeling up for dinner!" His expression is bright and happy. "They're serving lamb tonight. I think you'll like it. Would you like a drink before we sit?" His manners are impeccable, and I take him up on it.

"Yes, I'll have a glass of white wine." I really liked the mimosa from earlier, but he said it was a morning drink.

He orders a glass of white wine for each of us, and they come quickly. The service on this ship is impeccable. It's almost like they can anticipate your needs before you do.

"Salute!" he says. "Come, let's go sit at our table."

The dining room is amazing with dark blue walls and rich cherrywood. The chairs are big and comfortable, covered in tan fabric. Every table is covered with a white tablecloth and more dishes and glasses than I've ever seen on one table. I recognize the Italian music that the band is playing.

It feels incredibly luxurious, and I start to feel guilty. I wish Paola and my mother could see this, but my family is still in Orsara. In the last letter I got from them, they were thinking about moving to Chieri, too. I think it's a great idea, and they'll be able to make more money to save for the move to America.

The attendant brings us to our table for two, which has a small vase with flowers in the center. People are all flooding in around us, taking their seats in time for dinner service to begin.

David likes to talk. He tells me all about his trip and where he's been over the last couple of months. Then he talks about college and how much he enjoyed it. That part I'm very interested in. I want to go to college, too, someday, so I ask a lot of questions. I find out that he graduated with a degree in engineering. He already has a job when he gets back home.

Dinner was amazing, followed by dessert and coffee.

"Would you like an after-dinner drink? Maybe Strega?" David says. I remember seeing the yellow liqueur in bottles in the bar in my town, but I've never tried it.

"Sure, why not?" I say excited.

He orders it for me on the rocks, and when it comes, we salute again. It's very sweet and has a faint taste of mint and fennel. I like it a lot and have no trouble finishing the whole drink.

"Let's dance a little, what do you think?" David is definitely a lot of fun. He grabs my hand, and we get up and head to where the band is playing. We spend the rest of the evening dancing and talking like we've known each other forever. I knew my aunt was wrong about American men. I can already tell.

"David, thank you so much for such a lovely evening, but I think it's about time that I go back to my room. It was such a pleasure, really!" I hold out my hand to shake, and he gently pulls me in for a kiss on the cheek. It is very sweet, and I feel my face go pink with excitement.

"Thank you for a lovely evening. Hopefully we can do it again soon. I mean, we have at least five more chances, right?" He smiles and walks me to the dining room door and we part ways. This has been an evening that I know I will never forget.

The next morning, I wake up to the boat rocking violently from left to right. The queasy feeling I had on the first day is back with a vengeance. It feels like the sea must really be rough out there, and it goes on like this for a long time. I run several times to the bathroom to throw up again.

I don't have any water in my room, so I have to muster up enough energy to go out and get a few things. As soon as I leave my room, a crewman stops me and says it's safer if I stay inside. A big storm is brewing, and the seas are rough. I'll get thrown around if I try to go anywhere. He says he'll bring me some water and crackers for my seasickness, and I go back into my room.

This goes on for several days, and I feel like I'm going to die. It's so horrible being on this boat, all I want to do is get off. I'm trying to stay positive, but I break down and cry. I wish I could get something from the infirmary, but I'm afraid to leave my room.

I'm all alone.

I'm sick and I can't get away from it.

This is worse than I could have ever imagined.

I'm more miserable than I've ever been in my entire life.

It's my seventh morning on board. I wake up and the boat finally feels more stable, not moving side to side as much as before and definitely more tolerable for me. I look in the bathroom mirror and I don't even recognize myself. My face is pale and skinny, and my hair looks dull. I haven't eaten anything of substance since my dinner with David. I wonder how he is feeling.

I clean myself up and get dressed. I think fresh air might be a good idea since it worked last time. Besides, we must be getting close to New York, and I need to be around people.

I walk out to the welcome lounge and ask a crew member how much longer before we arrive.

"Tomorrow, miss. We'll be in port in New York Harbor tomorrow morning." He says as he continues with his work.

Oh thank goodness!

One last day on this ship before I get to land.

I think I can do it!

As long as we don't have another day like the last few.

I spend the day enjoying the boat for the last time. I go to the pool and see David there.

"Hey, I was worried about you! I would've checked on you, but I don't know where your room is. Were you okay during the rough seas?" David asks with concern.

"Oh, David I was so sick, as you can probably imagine. It was the most awful feeling I've ever had in my life. And it felt like it lasted forever. I think that was a pretty long storm," I say, suddenly feeling like I'm talking too much now.

"But I'm feeling okay now. How did you do?" I ask, wondering if the great seaman was able to keep it together during these last few days.

"Well I have to admit, I did feel a little queasy at times. But it was really rough!" He pushed it off as if it was no big deal.

We spend the afternoon chatting some more about ourselves. This time he seems a little more interested in what my life was like before this trip. I tell him about all my brothers and sisters and my little town, which of course he's never heard of. He seemed very intrigued by the fact that we didn't have a car.

"Well it's our last night on board. Should we have dinner again? I had a really nice time the other night." He asks sweetly.

"I would love that! I hear they have four o'clock teatime. I think I'm going to go have tea first and then I'll meet you in the dining room again if that's okay?" I say as I get up to walk away.

He gets up as well. "Yes, that sounds great, see you tonight."

Tea sounds really good right now. I think it's just what my stomach needs. I enjoy teatime with the other passengers and then go back to my cabin. It hits me that I'll be in New York City tomorrow, so I pull out my suitcase from under my bed and begin packing. I leave my pajamas and my pink suit out for tomorrow.

Dinner was even better than it was the other night. I think they save their best for the last night on board. So you don't remember all the bad days of rough seas. David asks if we can see each other once I get settled in America, but I can't think that far ahead.

"Oh David, I'm so unsure of my plans once I get to America. I have a lot of work to do once we arrive so I can move my family here. Let's definitely exchange information and keep in touch. I'd love to visit your town someday," I say enthusiastically.

"I understand. I will be starting my new job when I get home. It'll be intense work for the first few months, but I'd really like to keep in touch with you. I'd love to get to know you better," he says from the heart.

"I'd like that David." I say blushing a little.

I like the attention, but I have serious matters to consider. I'm so close now.

David and I exchange information so we can keep in touch, have one last sweet moment together, and then I head back to my room. I'm feeling elated and ready for anything to come. But for now, I'm so excited to go to sleep.

I go to bed feeling hopeful for what's to come.

I dream about my family, my parents, my brothers and sisters; all coming over to live with me in a regular house, with running water and bedrooms.

I dream about opportunity and the jobs that exist in America.

We can make a better life here; I just know it.

The next morning, I wake up and get dressed quickly. I fix my hair and look in the mirror. I see myself differently, and I already feel myself changing. My suitcase is packed, and I rush up to the main deck where I stood just eight days earlier and waved away my old life.

We're coming in slowly, and I can see the Statue of Liberty in front of me. Getting closer and closer. There she stands, an unbelievable sight to see. A calm presence as she towers over the harbor, she has a look of determination on her face that is unwavering. She is the face of hope, dreams, and infinite freedom.

Representing excitement for the future.

Standing proudly, ready for anything life gives.

Strong and ready to move forward into this new world.

We dock, and it takes some time to get off the boat and through customs. But when the time comes to take my first steps onto the sidewalk in New York City, my knees are weak and I feel like I'm about to cry, tears of joy.

I've finally arrived.

I'm finally home!

ACKNOWLEDGMENTS

———

I'd like to thank those who have given this book, and the stories within it, legs strong enough to stand on. You all invested so much time in helping me reach my goals and I am eternally grateful:

Antonietta Marinaccio Livorno, Leonardo Livorno, Damien Ramondo, Luke J. McMaster, Damien V. Ramondo and Giordan L. Ramondo

I'd also like to recognize the following people for believing in me, even before they could read my book:

Jacquelyn Abbey, Sue Addis, Chelsea Anderson, Sonya Aversa, Marjorie Bailey, Robin Bangle, Stephanie Bare, Carolyn Belveal, Alicia M. Bloch, Tre' Bohannon, Lisa Borowski, Nora Brady, JoAnn Buono, Maria Carpenter, Robert Catelli, Bonnie S Collyer, Cate Cox, Kristine Kessler Cox, Linda Criniti, A Roy DeCaro, Joanna Dibianca, Denise Max DiCarlo, Tonda H DiPasquale, Brenda Dunyan, Connie & William J. Eisenbrey, Robin Elliott, Jeanne Feliciani, Michele Ferrante, Aimee Gallagher, Allison Gamba, In Loving Memory of Jason Gamba, Michael Gambol, David and Lauren Geary, Gia Gentile, Lindsay Gersbach, Clare Girton, Susan Graham, Rosanna Hagg, Kim Hannum, Angela Hauber,

Nancy Healy, Allyson Henkel, Annie Hill, Barri Hill, Jennifer Holz, Tracy Hornbaker, Susan N Hunt, Megan Irish, Nancy Jameison, Olga Kanteliotis, Megen Karakelian, Julie Kelly, Arlene Kim, Jodie Klein, Eric Koester, Maria Krauss, Joanne LaSpada, Laura Lebaudy, Tracy Liebezeit, Valerie Lingo, Dieneke Lips, Ella Livorno, Joseph Livorno, Maria Livorno, Sam Livorno, Melyce Lucchesi, Carolyn MacMurtrie, MaryBeth Madonia, Sara Maggitti, Leonard Brian Marinaccio, Jennifer Marsh, Rotha Marsh, Sue Marsh, Anna Mazzola, Michael Mazzola, Jennifer McAleese, Gina Mchugh, Carole McKeon, Clara Meyers, Allison Miller, Kate Miller, Lisa Minakowski, Suzanne B Mitros, Kristin Monty, Lila Moran, Lisa Murphy, Adam Murray, Melissa Odorisio, Louis M. Onori Jr., Mary Ostien, Dana Ott, Deborah E. Palmer, Michela Palmer, Christine K Palus, Cherie Passarella, Denis Passarella, Pamela Perakis, Severn Perona, Amy Plumstead, Sharon Popik, Anthony Ramondo, Damien Ramondo, Carla Reid, Carol Rein, Kristen Ressler, Lon Rosenblum, Colleen M Ruane, Mara Sears, Shannon Selig, Maureen Sheridan, June Slowik, Rebecca Snyder, Deborah Sutton, Adele Terlizzi, Julie Tewksbury, Joanne Treadway, Laurie Turner, Kristin Van Dusen, Alexandra Vitale, Diane Vittorio, Amy Wallace, Lauren Webb, Nina Zodtner

Lastly, I'd like to acknowledge that this book would not have been possible without the tremendous insight and support from the following:

Rebecca Bruckenstein, Eric Koester, Melody Delgado Lorbeer, Mindy Thomas, The Creator's Institute, all my Georgetown friends, all the incredible staff and editors of New Degree Press and my interviewees.

Made in the USA
Las Vegas, NV
19 December 2023

83291509R00125